FIFTY-FIFTY

BOOK TWO

An Intermediate Course in Communicative English

Warren Wilson ◆ Roger Barnard

Prentice Hall Regents
Englewood Cliffs, New Jersey 07632

Editorial Director: Arley Gray
Acquisitions Editor: Nancy Baxer
Director of Production and Manufacturing: David Riccardi
Electronic Production Coordinator: Molly Pike Riccardi
Creative Director: Paula Maylahn

Editorial Production/Design Manager: Dominick Mosco
Electronic/Production Supervision, Page Composition,
    and Interior Design: Noël Vreeland Carter
Electronic Art: Rolando Corujo
Cover Design Coordinator: Merle Krumper
Cover Design: Amy Rosen
Production Coordinator: Ray Keating

Art by Roger Barnard

© 1995 by PRENTICE HALL REGENTS
Prentice-Hall, Inc.
A Simon & Schuster Company
Englewood Cliffs, New Jersey 07632

Printed in the United States of America
10 9 8 7 6 5 4 3 2 1

ISBN 0-13-287558-6

Prentice-Hall International (UK) Limited, *London*
Prentice-Hall of Australia Pty. Limited, *Sydney*
Prentice-Hall of Canada Inc. *Toronto*
Prentice-Hall Hispanoamericana, S.A., *Mexico*
Prentice-Hall of India Private Limited, *New Delhi*
Prentice-Hall of Japan, Inc. *Tokyo*
Simon & Schuster Asia Pte. Ltd., *Singapore*
Editora Prentice-Hall do Brasil, Ltda., *Rio de Janeiro*

CONTENTS

ACKNOWLEDGMENTS

We would like to thank the teachers and students at the following schools for their valuable help in developing and revising this material:

Athénée-Français, Tokyo
Community English Program, Teachers College, Columbia University, New York
Cosmopolitan Language Institute, Tokyo
English Language Institute, Queens College, New York
International English Language Institute, Hunter College, New York
Tokyo School of Business, Tokyo

We would also like to thank those at Prentice Hall Regents who have worked on this project, particularly our editor, Nancy Baxer and our production editor, Noël Vreeland Carter.

For Sook, Masako, Mia, and Sophie.

R. B.
W.W.
Tokyo/New York
May, 1994

TO THE TEACHER

Fifty-Fifty Book Two has been designed as a follow-up course to *Fifty-Fifty: A Basic Course in Communicative English,* but it can be used independently in classes at the intermediate level. Designed primarily for use in large classes where "student-talking" time is usually very limited, the book can be used just as effectively in virtually any size class since it allows students to participate actively in meaningful exchanges in pair work and group work activities.

Fifty-Fifty Book Two concentrates on listening and speaking proficiency. It provides a wide variety of listening tasks as well as creative pair work and group work exercises, all of which are designed to reduce learner anxiety and promote language acquisition via student participation in purposeful communication and feedback. The book is intended for students who have a solid foundation in English and a fairly good passive knowledge of grammar and vocabulary, but lack the skills and confidence to converse freely in English.

The text consists of a warm-up unit, twelve main units, and three review units. Every fifth unit consolidates and recycles the material covered in the preceding units. The appendix contains the *Student B* pages of the pair work activities as well as the tapescript for the listening tasks.

Each unit provides the students with a brief presentation of the language point to be practiced, a listening task centered around the language point, and extensive oral/aural practice in which the students use the language purposefully and effectively. Every unit also contains a homework section that provides written practice in the material covered, thus reinforcing spelling and vocabulary as well as further demonstrating the language in context.

The five sections of each unit are described below. (The formats of the warm-up and review units differ slightly.)

PREVIEW

Each unit begins with a brief introductory task in the form of one or two comic sketches. Each sketch has one empty speech balloon to be filled in by the student. The sketches illustrate the unit theme and introduce, in a simple context, the language to be practiced.

Following the comic sketches is a language model that the students can study, practice, and refer to during the exercise. The questions and answers in the model can be used for pronunciation and intonation practice via choral repetition—i.e., the students repeating in unison after the teacher. The language model can also be expanded on the board with additional examples and be used as a base for substitution drilling.

The brief question-and-answer practice following the language model serves as a warm-up exercise. The class can practice the questions orally (teacher to student or student to student) or write out the questions and answers in their notebooks.

The *Teacher's Edition* provides additional suggestions as well as helpful hints for classroom use.

LISTENING TASK

The second section is an aural comprehension exercise that helps the students focus on the particular language point to be practiced. The students are not expected to retain or reproduce all the language they hear on the tape, but their comprehension will increase as they focus on the information needed to complete the task. Generally, it is a good idea for the teacher to play the tape straight through first to familiarize the students with the content, then again with pauses as the students complete the task, and once more straight through as they check their answers. After the teacher has elicited the answers from the class, the students can listen to the tape a final time, perhaps while going over the tapescript. A subsequent question-and-answer exchange—teacher to student or student to student—could provide additional practice.

The tapescript for the Listening Tasks are located in the appendix and can be utilized for extended practice and/or review. The *Teacher's Edition* provides helpful hints, as well as the answers, to ensure that the exercise goes smoothly. Ideas for extended practice are also included for most Listening Tasks.

PAIR WORK

The Pair Work section provides communicative practice that maximizes classroom "student talking" time. The exercise is designed to elicit specific queries and responses; each student completes the task by asking his or her partner for missing information. Being task-based, the exercise provides more than just question-and-answer practice: actual communication takes place—that is, the completion of each task relies on a real exchange of information and feedback.

In most units, the language model in the Preview section serves as a guide for the Pair Work activity. Certain tasks, however, require additional language or call for a slightly different type of exchange (for example, a "yes/no" question instead of a "wh~" question). It is up to the teacher to make sure that the students (a) understand the directions, (b) practice the language pattern sufficiently beforehand, and (c) have a guide to refer to (such as a language model on the board). In addition, it is always helpful to demonstrate the exercise with a good student. The *Teacher's Edition* provides suggestions for warm-up exercises and extended practice.

The students should sit face to face, if possible, and maintain eye contact while speaking. Whenever possible, they should alternate asking and answering, even if it is slower. They should never look at each other's pages and should always ask for spelling or repetition in English.

The teacher can circulate through the class, monitoring the students individually and assisting those who need help. It is advisable to circulate once quickly at the outset to make sure that everyone has gotten off to a good start. Correction techniques vary from teacher to teacher and exercise to exercise; however, during communicative practice it is usually advisable to leave correction until afterwards. The point of the tasks is communication, not the production of flawless sentences. (Nevertheless, major errors that are counterproductive to the practice can and should be rectified whenever necessary.)

Finally, the teacher can check the finished work by looking at the students' textbooks and briefly querying their partners for verification. Students can also confer and check the work themselves. Any problems or error correction can be gone over with the class at this time. (At a later date the task can be repeated for a quick review by utilizing the students' unused *Student A* and *Student B* pages.)

GROUP WORK

The Group Work activities, by their very nature, involve more class interaction than the Pair Work activities, and usually demand more spontaneous communication because of the faster pace and frequent changing of partners. Group Work exercises include "find someone who" activities, group interviews, and various types of language games that promote meaningful interaction while lessening learner anxiety.

All suggestions given above for the Pair Work section apply to this section; the recommended procedures are the same. However, many activities in the Group Work section require that the students move around the classroom. The teacher should make sure that everyone gets up and circulates, however reluctant they may be at first.

In the review units, the Group Work section is followed by a section entitled Language Game. This activity involves competition between students in a group, or between teams, and ends with one student (or team) as the winner. The point of the game is to provide ample comprehensible input regarding vocabulary and structures from the preceding units, and involves a mnemonic device to help students retain what they hear. The *Teacher's Edition* outlines alternative ways of conducting the Language Game.

HOMEWORK

The last section is designed to be a homework assignment but can be used in class when appropriate, by students working alone or in pairs. The teacher can also have the students do the assignment on a separate sheet of paper to be handed in. The *Teacher's Edition* contains answers for the Homework section (though alternatives are always possible) and provides additional suggestions for classroom use.

PREVIEW

1. The following conversation takes place after the first Japanese class at a university in New York. Practice the conversation with a partner.

Student A:	Hello. I'm Paul Savage.
Student B:	Nice to meet you. My name's Jane, Jane Spencer.
Student A:	Glad to meet you, Jane. Where are you from?
Student B:	I'm from San Francisco, but now I live in New Jersey. What do you do, Paul?
Student A:	Right now I'm studying law here at Columbia. How about you?
Student B:	I'm a software designer. I work for Nintendo.
Student A:	Oh, really? So why are you studying Japanese?
Student B:	Well, I'm going to work in our Tokyo office next year. And you?
Student A:	Oh, just for fun, I guess.

2. Practice the above conversation again, this time using information about yourself. (Use *true* information if you can, or make something up.)

○ Memo ○
• ALWAYS MAKE EYE CONTACT WHEN YOU SPEAK WITH SOMEONE— DON'T LOOK DOWN AT THE PAGE!

3. Practice the conversation one more time with a new partner, again using information about yourself. This time, ask some of the questions below, as well as a few questions of your own.

What do you think of <u>New York</u>**?**	**I really like it.**
What do you like doing in your free time?	**I like** <u>going to the movies</u>**.**
What kind of <u>music</u> **do you like?**	**I love** <u>classical music</u>**.**
Can you speak <u>German</u>**?**	**Yeah, but only a little.**
What other languages can you speak?	**I can speak** <u>Spanish</u>**, and a little** <u>Greek</u>**.**

LISTENING TASK

Listen to the conversation and check (√) all the correct information for John and Maria.

	is from Denver	is from Chicago	lives in Denver	lives in Chicago	is a teacher	is a tour guide	is a graphic designer	goes to art shows	can speak Italian	can speak French
JOHN	☐	☐	☐	☐	☐	☐	☐	☐	☐	☐
MARIA	☐	☐	☐	☐	☐	☐	☐	☐	☐	☐

PAIR WORK

STUDENT B:
LOOK AT
PAGE 92

1. Take turns with *Student B* asking and answering questions, and fill in the blanks in the three paragraphs below (1 through 3).

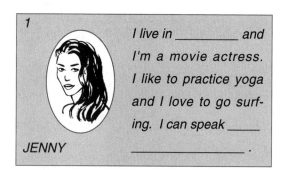

1
JENNY

I live in _____ and I'm a movie actress. I like to practice yoga and I love to go surfing. I can speak _____ _____ .

2
PHIL

I'm a _____ . In my free time I _____ _____ . I live in Berlin and I can speak German and French fluently.

3
HARRY
& LISA

We are both _____ and we live in _____ . We both can speak Japanese and we love to go hiking and camping whenever we can.

4

STUDENT
B
- - - - - - - - -
name

_____
_____
_____
_____
_____
_____

2. Take turns with *Student B* asking and answering questions, and write a short paragraph like the others about *Student B* in box number 4.

GROUP WORK

1. Fill in each blank below with fictional information from the box on the right.
(Use this information to answer questions in number 2.)

Your residence: _____
Your occupation: _____
Languages you speak: _____
Your hobby: _____

2. Walk around the room and ask questions. Find someone with the same information for at least *three* of the items. Check (√) the three items and write his or her name below.

☐
☐
☐   - - - - - - - - - - - - - - - - - - -
☐   *name*

- *New Orleans*
- *Munich*
- *Singapore*

- *travel writer*
- *artist*
- *hotel manager*

- *two languages*
- *three languages*
- *six languages*

- *horseback riding*
- *hang gliding*
- *rollerblading*

PREVIEW

I'd like some information about <u>the train to Miami</u>.	Sure. How can I help you?

Do you know	what time <u>it leaves</u>?	It leaves at 10:55 in the morning.
	how long <u>it takes</u>?	It takes one and a half hours.
Could you tell me	how much <u>it costs</u>?	One-way is $20, and round-trip is $35.
	if you have <u>anything cheaper</u>?	No, we don't have anything cheaper.

Look at the signs below (1 through 5). Ask and answer questions like the ones above with a partner.

1	2	3	4	5

Movie Times

1:50   6:10

4:00   8:20

Parking Rates

$1.50 per hour
$10 for 8 hours
$14 all day

Guided Tours

Start	Finish
11:00	12:30
1:00	2:30
3:00	4:30

TOLL

$3.00 cars
$2.00 motorcycles
$7.50 trucks

Ferry

Dep:
1:00, 3:00, 5:30

Arr:
2:30, 4:30, 8:00

LISTENING TASK

○ Memo ○
• YOU ONLY HEAR
ONE SIDE OF EACH
PHONE CONVERSATION.
• EXERCISE 2 CAN BE
DONE WITH A PARTNER OR
IN A SMALL GROUP.

EXERCISE 1

Listen to the conversations (1 through 4) and write
the number of each conversation on the correct picture.

EXERCISE 2

Listen to each conversation again. After each one write
down any questions that you can remember.

PAIR WORK

STUDENT B:
LOOK AT
PAGE 93

EXERCISE 1

You are going to take a bus trip from New York City to another city.
Choose *where* you want to go and *when* you want to leave:

You want to go to   ❑ *Miami.*
                       ❑ *Denver.*

You want to leave on ❑ *Monday,*
                       ❑ *Thursday,*
                       ❑ *Friday,*

at about   ___*o'clock*

in the   ❑ *morning.*
              ❑ *afternoon.*
              ❑ *evening.*

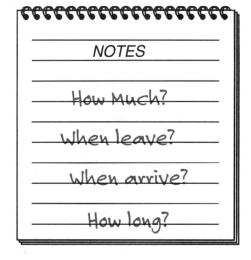

NOTES

How Much?

When leave?

When arrive?

How long?

Student B works at the Port Authority Bus Terminal.
Ask *Student B* questions and write the answers in the notebook.

NEW YORK PENN STATION TRAIN INFORMATION		
DESTINATION:	*CHICAGO*	*L.A.*
FARE:	*$135*	*$247*
	Departs Arrives	Departs Arrives
	10:00 5:15	10:00 9:30
DAILY	11:15 6:30	11:15 10:45
DEPARTURE	12:45 8:00	12:45 12:15
AND	14:00 9:15	14:00 13:30
ARRIVAL	15:30 10:45	15:30 15:00
TIMES:	17:15 12:30	17:15 16:45
	19:45 15:00	19:45 19:15
	21:30 16:45	21:30 21:00
ARRIVAL DAY:	*+ one day*	*+ two days*
TRAVEL TIME:	*18 hrs. 15 min.*	*44 hrs. 30 min.*

EXERCISE 2

You are a train reservation clerk at New York Penn Station.
Look at the train schedule and answer *Student B's* questions.

EXERCISE 3

You are the manager of a language school.
Student B wants to take a language course.
Answer *Student B's* questions.
(Make up the answers!)

EXAMPLE:
STUDENT B: *"Could you tell me if you have a Chinese course?"*
STUDENT A: *"Yes, we do."*

➤ *STUDENT A and STUDENT B: Change roles and do Exercise 3 again!*

GROUP WORK

Choose *one* of the boxes below (pages 8~9). Walk around the classroom and ask for information and give information. Write the answer next to each question.

○ Memo ○

• THE TEACHER MAY GIVE YOU A BOX.
• ALL OF THE BOXES ON ONE OR BOTH OF THE PAGES MUST BE USED.

1

Find someone who knows:

• how long it takes to go from England to France by ferry. _____
• how much it costs to go from England to France by ferry. _____
• the best time of the year to visit Greece.

_____

Give the following information to anyone who asks for it.

• A train ticket from Tokyo to Osaka for the *bullet train* costs about $125.
• Two places to visit in San Francisco are the Golden Gate Bridge and Fisherman's Wharf.
• It takes about 3 1/2 hours to fly from Australia to New Zealand.

2

Find someone who knows:

• how much it costs to take a horse-and-buggy ride in Central Park in New York City. _____
• the cheapest way to travel from New York to California. _____
• where to go sightseeing in San Francisco.

_____

Give the following information to anyone who asks for it.

• It takes about 1 1/2 hours to go from England to France by ferry.
• It takes about 2 1/2 hours to go from Tokyo to Osaka by the *bullet train*.
• It's cold in Australia in July. (It's winter!)

3

Find someone who knows:

• how long it takes to travel by train from Tokyo to Osaka. _____
• how much it costs to travel by train from Tokyo to Osaka. _____
• what time most of the subways stop running in Tokyo. _____

Give the following information to anyone who asks for it.

• Springtime is the best time of the year to visit Greece.
• January is the best month to travel through Australia.
• The cheapest way to travel from New York to California is by bus.

4

Find someone who knows:

• the best month to travel through Australia. _____
• what the weather is like in Australia in July. _____
• how long it takes to fly from Australia to New Zealand. _____

Give the following information to anyone who asks for it.

• A ferry ticket costs about $50 one way from England to France.
• Most of the subways in Tokyo stop running about one o'clock in the morning.
• It costs about $40 to take a horse-and-buggy ride in Central Park in New York City.

5

Find someone who knows:

• what the weather is like in India in August.

_____

• what the weather is like in Thailand in January.

_____

• what time the banks open in the morning in Hong Kong.

_____

- -

*Give the following information
to anyone who asks for it.*

• A cup of coffee costs about $3.50 at a sidewalk cafe in Paris.
• Springtime is the best season to trek in the Himalayas.
• It costs about $350 round trip for a discount flight from New York to London.

6

Find someone who knows:

• how long it takes to fly from New York to London.

_____

• how much it costs to fly from New York to London.

_____

• how much it costs to see a movie in London.

_____

- -

*Give the following information
to anyone who asks for it.*

• Most of the shops in Barcelona are closed for *siesta* from 1:30 to 3:30 in the afternoon.
• The best way to travel from Hong Kong to Macau is by *jetfoil*, the fastest ferry.
• It's very hot in Thailand in January.

7

Find someone who knows:

• the best way to travel from Hong Kong to Macau.

_____

• where to go sightseeing in Beijing, China.

_____

• the best season to trek in the Himalayas.

_____

- -

*Give the following information
to anyone who asks for it.*

• The banks in Hong Kong open at nine o'clock in the morning.
• It takes about 7 1/2 hours to fly from New York to London.
• Two places to visit in Athens are the Plaka and the Parthenon.

8

Find someone who knows:

• how much a cup of coffee costs at a sidewalk cafe in Paris.

_____

• what time the shops are closed for *siesta* in Barcelona, Spain.

_____

• where to go sightseeing in Athens, Greece.

_____

- -

*Give the following information
to anyone who asks for it.*

• It's hot and rainy in India in August.

• It costs about $8.00 to see a movie in London.

• Two places to visit in Beijing are the Great Wall and the Forbidden City.

HOMEWORK

In each of the situations below, one person is getting information from another person. Write a question and answer for each of the situations.

○ Memo ○

• WRITE A DIFFERENT QUESTION EACH TIME.

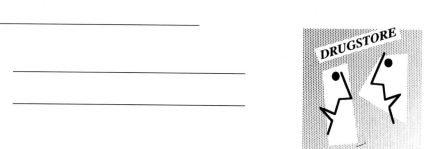

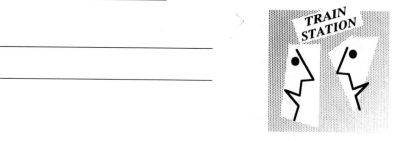

_____

_____

_____

_____

_____

_____

_____

_____

_____

_____

_____

_____

2 IT'S BLACK AND WHITE

PREVIEW

What does it look like?	It's <u>small</u> **and** <u>square</u>. It's <u>black</u> **and it has** <u>stripes</u>. **It has** <u>a zipper</u>.
What is it made of?	**It's made of** <u>leather</u>.

VOCABULARY

• round	• wood
• flowers	• dark blue
• long	• large
• buttons	• cotton
• polka dots	• pinkish
• pocket-size	• handle
• flat	• gray and white
• pocket	• plastic
• checks	• medium-sized

1. Fill in the boxes below with the appropriate words from the vocabulary box on the right. Then work with a partner and add two words of your own to each box.

2. Take turns with a partner describing objects in the classroom.

SIZE	*SHAPE*	*COLOR*	*PATTERN*	*FEATURES*	*MATERIAL*

LISTENING TASK

EXERCISE 1

Read each sentence (*a* through *o*) and write the letter below each item that it describes.

a) It's made of leather.
b) It has a handle.
c) It's black.
d) It has buttons.
e) It's made mostly of plastic.

f) It has a little plastic window.
g) It's brown.
h) It's plain, with almost no design.
i) It has batteries.
j) It has switches.

k) It has a strap.
l) There are numbers on it.
m) It has a lock.
n) It's made of wood.
o) It's square.

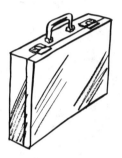

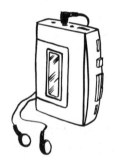

EXERCISE 2

1. Listen to the conversations (1 through 6) and
write the number of each conversation above the correct item.

2. Listen again and write the *key words* next to each item.

PAIR WORK

Student A:

1. Choose eight different items and write numbers
1 through 8 on them.

2. Describe each item to *Student B*.

Student B:

Listen to *Student A* describe eight items.
Write the number (1 through 8) on each one.
Ask questions to be sure!

○ Memo ○
• DO NOT MENTION THE
ITEMS BY NAME, OR WHAT
THEY ARE USED FOR.
• DO NOT LOOK AT
YOUR PARTNER'S PAGE: ASK
QUESTIONS TO CHECK ANSWERS.

GARAGE SALE TODAY!

→ *Student A and Student B: Change roles and do the exercise again!*

Work in groups of four.

Student A:

Choose one object from one of the rooms below (pages 14~15). Don't tell the other students inyour group—they will ask you questions and try to find out which object it is. Answer all questions with "Yes" or "No".

○ Memo ○

• DO THIS EXERCISE
FOUR TIMES:
EACH STUDENT TAKE
A TURN AS STUDENT A.

Students B, C, & D:

Ask *Student A* "yes/no" questions and try to find out which object *Student A* has chosen. Whoever guesses the object first wins. You can't ask more than twenty questions.

If no one can guess it, Student A *wins!*

○ Memo ○
• TAKE TURNS ASKING QUESTIONS.
• BE CAREFUL—IF YOU GUESS THE WRONG OBJECT, YOU'RE OUT!

TYPES OF 'YES/NO' QUESTIONS

• *Is it usually found in <u>the kitchen</u>?*
• *Do you use it <u>often</u>?*
• *Is it <u>small</u>?*
• *Does it have a <u>handle</u>?*
• *Is it made of <u>plastic</u>?*

HOMEWORK

Find a large picture of an interesting object in a magazine or newspaper.
Cut out the picture and tape it on this page.
Write a description of the object on the lines below.

TAPE PICTURE HERE

_____

_____

_____

_____

_____

_____

_____

_____

_____

_____

_____

3 WOULD YOU MIND?

PREVIEW

Can you <u>close the door</u>?
Could you <u>lend me your pen</u>?

Do you think you could <u>call me tonight</u>?
Could you possibly <u>meet me after school</u>?

Would it be possible for you to <u>help me move this weekend</u>?
I was wondering if you could possibly <u>take me to the airport</u>.

Would you mind <u>turning down the volume</u>?

Sure.

Of course.

I'd be glad to.

No problem.

Not at all.

I'm afraid I can't.

I'm sorry, but <u>I'm really busy</u>.

I wish I could, but...

Look at the pictures (1 through 5). Ask and answer the above questions with a partner.

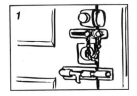    

LISTENING TASK

EXERCISE 1

Listen to the conversation and circle the things that Julie asks Larry to do.

EXERCISE 2

Listen again and check (√) all the things that Larry agrees to do.

EXERCISE 3

Listen once more and make an "**X**" on the things that Larry agrees to do, but doesn't really *want* to do.

PAIR WORK

1. Make an "**X**" on six of the things below that you would rather *not* do for your partner.
   (Don't show your partner which six things you have chosen.)
   For each one, think of a reason not to do it if asked.

2. With a partner, take turns asking each other to do things.
   You must agree to do anything not marked with an "**X**".

The first one to get his or her partner to say 'Yes' to six requests is the winner!

○ Memo ○

• ALWAYS GIVE A
<u>REASON</u> WHEN YOU
REFUSE A REQUEST.

GROUP WORK

Choose *one* of the boxes below (pages 20~21). Walk around the classroom and ask others to do things for you, and agree—or refuse—to do things for others. Write the name of the person who agrees to do something next to the request.

○ Memo ○

• THE TEACHER MAY GIVE YOU A BOX.
• ALL OF THE BOXES ON ONE OR BOTH OF THE PAGES MUST BE USED.

1

Find someone who will:

• drive you to the airport tomorrow evening.
_____

• baby-sit your little brother tonight.
_____

• let you copy yesterday's class notes.
_____

- -

Agree to:

• pick up some books at the library.

• lend your friend ten dollars.

• take care of your friend's cat this summer.

Refuse all other requests!

2

Find someone who will:

• lend you ten dollars.
_____

• help you look for your dog today.
_____

• water your house plants while you're away next weekend.
_____

- -

Agree to:

• let your friend copy your class notes.

• carry some boxes downstairs.

• go to the post office for your friend.

Refuse all other requests!

3

Find someone who will:

• help you with the homework after school.
_____

• take care of your cat for a month this summer.
_____

• go to the post office and mail some letters for you right away.
_____

- -

Agree to:

• teach your friend how to use the school computer lab.
• water your friend's house plants.

• baby-sit your friend's little brother.

Refuse all other requests!

4

Find someone who will:

• teach you how to use the school computer lab after class.
_____
• pick up some books for you at the library this afternoon.
_____
• carry some boxes downstairs for you.
_____

- -

Agree to:

• drive your friend to the airport.

• look for your friend's dog.

• help your friend with the homework.

Refuse all other requests!

5

Find someone who will:

• lend you a dictionary.

_____

• pick up your laundry tomorrow morning.

_____

• help you paint your kitchen this afternoon.

_____

- -

Agree to:

• lend your friend a videocamera.

• let your friend copy your homework.

• show your friend how to program a new VCR.

Refuse all other requests!

6

Find someone who will:

• let you copy the homework due today.

_____

• help you move to a new house on Sunday.

_____

• feed your goldfish while you're on vacation next week.

_____

- -

Agree to:

• lend your friend a dictionary.

• go to the bank for your friend.

• go to the supermarket for your friend.

Refuse all other requests!

7

Find someone who will:

• help you fix your car.

_____

• show you how to program your new VCR.

_____

• go to the supermarket for you.

_____

- -

Agree to:

• explain the class project to your friend.

• feed your friend's goldfish.

• pick up your friend's laundry.

Refuse all other requests!

8

Find someone who will:

• explain the class project to you after school.

_____

• lend you a videocamera for a week.

_____

• go to the bank for you right away.

_____

- -

Agree to:

• help paint your friend's kitchen.

• help your friend move to a new house.

• help fix your friend's car.

Refuse all other requests!

HOMEWORK

EXERCISE 1

Match the pictures with the dialogs and write a request in each of the dialogs.

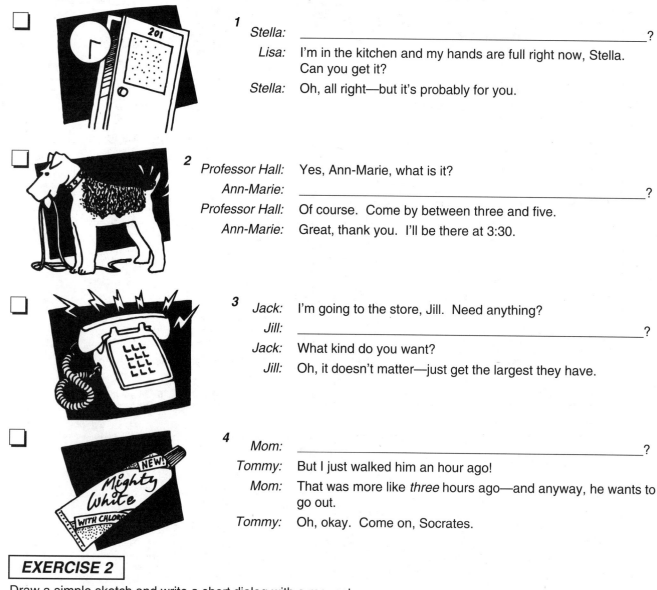

☐

1
Stella: _____?
Lisa: I'm in the kitchen and my hands are full right now, Stella. Can you get it?
Stella: Oh, all right—but it's probably for you.

☐

2
Professor Hall: Yes, Ann-Marie, what is it?
Ann-Marie: _____?
Professor Hall: Of course. Come by between three and five.
Ann-Marie: Great, thank you. I'll be there at 3:30.

☐

3
Jack: I'm going to the store, Jill. Need anything?
Jill: _____?
Jack: What kind do you want?
Jill: Oh, it doesn't matter—just get the largest they have.

☐

4
Mom: _____?
Tommy: But I just walked him an hour ago!
Mom: That was more like *three* hours ago—and anyway, he wants to go out.
Tommy: Oh, okay. Come on, Socrates.

EXERCISE 2

Draw a simple sketch and write a short dialog with a request.

_____
_____
_____
_____

4 TURN IT CLOCKWISE

PREVIEW

How can I How do you Could you tell me how to	buy a ticket?

First, find your station on the map and put your money in.
Then, push the button for the ticket amount.
After that, take your ticket and change from the machine.

1. Match the instructions on how to use an ATM (*Automated Teller Machine*) with the pictures (1 through 6).

☐ *Take out the money and count it.*

☐ *Enter the amount you want and push the "ENTER" button.*

☐ *Take out your cash card and insert it into the cash machine.*

☐ *Push the button that says "WITHDRAWAL."*

☐ *Take your card out of the machine and put it away.*

☐ *Enter your identification number and push the "ENTER" button.*

1.    2.

3.    4.

5. 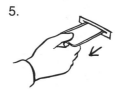   6.

2. Practice giving and following the instructions with a partner.

LISTENING TASK

EXERCISE 1

Listen to six short conversations between a flight attendant
and two passengers and write the number of each conversation
(1 through 6) on the correct picture.

EXERCISE 2

Listen to six short conversations between the two passengers,
a husband and wife, and on each of the pictures (1 through 6),
write "**H**" if the husband is right, or "**W**" if the wife is right.

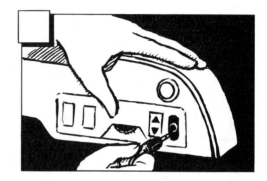

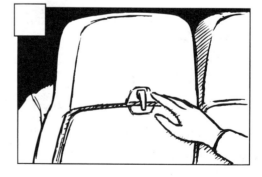

EXERCISE 3

Make a note of the instructions for each picture (1 through 6), and then compare notes with a partner.

PAIR WORK

EXERCISE 1

The teacher will divide the class into pairs, and assign each pair a set of pictures from pages 25~26 (*A, B, C, or D*).
Each pair should work together and write down directions for their set of pictures.

A

_____   _____   _____

_____   _____   _____

_____   _____   _____

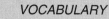

_____   _____   _____

_____   _____   _____

_____   _____   _____

VOCABULARY	
• lid (or cover)	• select
• face down	• push (or press)
• glass	• start button

B

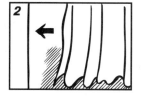

_____   _____   _____

_____   _____   _____

_____   _____   _____

_____   _____   _____

VOCABULARY	
• adjust	• photo size
• curtain	• insert (or put in)
• select	• tray

EXERCISE 2

For each of the *other* three sets of pictures, walk around the classroom and find someone to give you the instructions, and write them below the pictures.

(Only *give* instructions for *your* set of pictures.)

Afterwards, compare your answers with your partner's answers.

Memo
• ASK FOR AND GIVE INSTRUCTIONS BY YOURSELF IN EXERCISE 2.
• LOOK AT THE PICTURES WHEN YOU GIVE OR RECEIVE INSTRUCTIONS—DON'T READ!

 **1**

 **2**

 **3**

_____

_____

_____

 **4**

 **5**

 **6**

_____

_____

_____

C

VOCABULARY	
• nozzle	• insert
• gas pump	• gas tank
• lever	• replace

D

 **1**

 **2**

 **3**

_____

_____

_____

4 WASH TEMP.
WARM   COLD
HOT

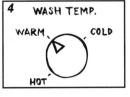 **5**

 **6**

_____

_____

_____

VOCABULARY	
• laundry	• detergent
• door	• select (or set)
• pour	• insert (or put in)

GROUP WORK

EXERCISE 1

In groups of three, practice doing the actions in the box, and then think up six more actions and add them to the list.

ACTIONS		
crawl	pinch	squeeze
cry	point at	throw
frown	pound on	tickle
grab	pull	turn around
hug	punch	wave to
jump	push	wink at
kick	scare	_____
kneel	scratch	_____
knock	shake	_____
look at	skip	_____
open	slap	_____
pick up	smile	_____

EXERCISE 2

Form *new* groups of three, and write a *silent movie scene* for two people (*Student A* and *Student B*) who will each complete six or more actions during the scene.
(Use actions from the box above or make up your own.)

EXAMPLE:
Student A: Point at the window and push <u>Student B</u>.
Student B: Go to the window and wink at <u>Student A</u>.
Student A: Go and stand behind <u>Student B</u>, turn around, and cry.

EXERCISE 3

Again, form new groups of three. Take turns being the *director* of the movie scene that you wrote in *EXERCISE 2*, giving instructions to the two *actors/actresses* (*Student A* and *Student B*).

EXAMPLE:
DIRECTOR: "Carla, point at the window and push Michael."
CARLA: [Points at the window and pushes Michael.]
DIRECTOR: "Good. Now, Michael, go to the window and wink at Carla."
MICHAEL: [Goes to the window and winks at Carla.]
DIRECTOR: "Okay. Carla, go and stand behind Michael, turn around, and cry."

HOMEWORK

EXERCISE 1

Unscramble the instructions below. Then write the correct instructions below each New York subway sign (1~6).

instructions from listen crew for
lean do doors on not
stay car in
cars not ride do between
pull brake do emergency not
onto straps hand hold

_____
_____
_____
_____
_____
_____

• IN AN EMERGENCY:

1

_____
_____

2

_____
_____

3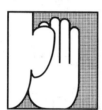

_____
_____

• WHILE TRAIN IS MOVING:

4

_____
_____

5

_____
_____

6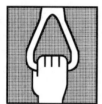

_____
_____

EXERCISE 2

Write instructions for each subway sign.

• AT ALL TIMES:

1

_____
_____

2

_____
_____

3

(Draw your own sign)

_____
_____

Policeman: Excuse me, Ma'am? Did you call 911?

Shop owner: Yes, I did. _____

_____?

Policeman: Oh, one of your little pets got out of the cage, huh? Sure, we can help you look. What does it look like?

Shop owner: _____

_____

_____

_____.

Shop owner: I guess you can start looking in the basement, Officer. ...Officer?

Customer: _____

Salesman: VCRs? Sure. What would you like to know?

Customer: _____

_____?

Salesman: That model? You just open this lid, press "Progam", then select either EP, LP or SP for the speed, and press "Check set." After that enter the date of the show, pressing "Check set" after each item, then the time, again pressing "Check set", and then press "Program" again—

Customer: Oh, never mind. I think I'm going to buy a toaster instead.

LISTENING TASK

1. Listen to the conversations (1 through 5) and write the number
of each conversation on the correct picture.

2. Listen again and write the *key words* next to each picture.

Student A:

1. Choose any twelve objects in the office above and number them from 1 to 12.

2. Describe each object to *Student B,* and tell *Student B* how to use it. (Do not say what the object is or what the object is used for.) Talk about each object until *Student B* guesses what it is.

⟶ **STUDENT A** and **STUDENT B**: *Change roles and do the exercise again!*

Student B:

Student A will describe twelve objects in the office, one at a time, and tell you how to use each one. Ask questions and guess what each one is.

○ Memo ○
• BOTH STUDENTS CAN CHOOSE 12 OBJECTS AT THE SAME TIME, AND TAKE TURNS DESCRIBING AND GUESSING.

1. Circle any four of the things below: *these are things you don't have and <u>want to borrow</u>.*
Make an "**X**" on four other things: *these are things you have, but <u>do not want to lend</u> to anyone.*
Leave four of the things unmarked: *these are things you have and <u>can lend</u>.*

2. Walk around the classroom and try to borrow the four things you circled above.
Refuse to lend the things you marked with an "**X**", and give a reason for refusing.
Lend each unmarked thing only one time—to the first person who asks you for it.
Write down the name of each person you lend something to or borrow something from.

LANGUAGE GAME

CALLER:
LOOK AT
PAGE 34

Play this game with two to six "players" and one "caller."

Take turns choosing two numbers (1 through 24) from the grid below.
Each number is a question or an answer. The caller will read each sentence that you choose.
Choose one number, listen to the caller read the sentence, and then choose another number.
Try to match a question with the answer. If you get a match, you get one extra turn (only) to choose again!

Do not write any notes—*just listen!*

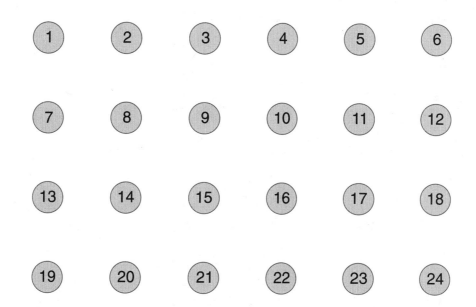

Continue until all the questions and answers have been matched.
The player with the most matches is the *winner!*

○ Memo ○

• CHECK (✓) THE NUMBERS
  THAT YOU MATCH.
• CROSS OFF (✗) THE
  NUMBERS THAT
  ANOTHER PLAYER MATCHES.

LANGUAGE GAME

PLAYERS:
LOOK AT
PAGE 33

Play this game with two to six "players" and one "caller."

1. Number the questions and answers below from 1 to 24 in *random order* (i.e., all mixed up).

2. The players will take turns choosing pairs of numbers.
Read aloud each of the two sentences that the player chooses, one at a time.
(The player will choose a second number <u>after</u> you read the first sentence.)
- If the two sentences *match,* shout "Match!" and write the player's name next to the sentences.
Then the same player gets one extra turn to choose two more numbers.
After that, the next player chooses.
- If the two sentences *do not match,* say "No match," and the next player chooses two numbers.

Question:	*Answer:*	*Player's name:*
◯ *Could you lend me your pen?*	◯ *Of course—here you are.*	_____
◯ *Could you tell me how long the trip is?*	◯ *It takes about 48 hours.*	_____
◯ *What does your jacket look like?*	◯ *Well, it's plaid and it has black buttons.*	_____
◯ *How do you use this ticket machine?*	◯ *Put in the money and press this button.*	_____
◯ *Do you know what time it leaves?*	◯ *Every hour on the hour.*	_____
◯ *What is that made of?*	◯ *Mostly glass, but this part is plastic.*	_____
◯ *Do you think you could give me a ride?*	◯ *Sure, no problem—it's on my way home.*	_____
◯ *How can I make a call on this phone?*	◯ *First dial "9" and then the phone number.*	_____
◯ *Where can I cash traveller's checks?*	◯ *There's a bank around the corner.*	_____
◯ *Do you know how to close this?*	◯ *Yeah, just turn it clockwise.*	_____
◯ *Would you mind calling me back later?*	◯ *Not at all—I'll call around five o'clock.*	_____
◯ *Is it big?*	◯ *No, it's small enough to fit in your pocket.*	_____

Continue until all the questions and answers are matched.
The player with the most matches is the *winner!*

○ Memo ○

- READ EACH SENTENCE
SLOWLY, NO MORE
THAN TWO TIMES.
- PLAYERS MUST
NOT LOOK AT THIS PAGE!

6 GO RIGHT AHEAD

PREVIEW

Okay if I <u>sit down</u>?

Can I <u>leave now</u>?
Could I <u>borrow a pen</u>?

Is it okay if I <u>use your phone</u>?
Is it all right if I <u>stay home</u>?

I wonder if I could <u>borrow your camera</u>?

Would it be possible for me to <u>use your car</u>?

Mind if I <u>come in</u>?

Do you mind if I <u>watch TV</u>?

Sure.
Sure, go ahead.
Of course.

Not at all.
No, go ahead.
No, please do.

Well, I'd rather you didn't.

Sorry, I'm afraid that <u>I have to use it</u>.

I'm sorry, but <u>it doesn't work</u>.

Look at the pictures (1 through 5). Ask and answer the above questions with a partner.

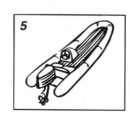

LISTENING TASK

EXERCISE 1

Listen to the conversations (1 through 10) and write the number of each conversation on the correct picture.

EXERCISE 2

Listen to each conversation again. For each one (1 through 10), make a check (√) in the box for *Permission given* or *Permission refused*.

	Permission: given	refused	Request: formal	informal
1.	☐	☐	☐	☐
2.	☐	☐	☐	☐
3.	☐	☐	☐	☐
4.	☐	☐	☐	☐
5.	☐	☐	☐	☐
6.	☐	☐	☐	☐
7.	☐	☐	☐	☐
8.	☐	☐	☐	☐
9.	☐	☐	☐	☐
10.	☐	☐	☐	☐

EXERCISE 3

Listen to each conversation once more. For each one (1 through 10), make a check (√) in the box for *formal* or *informal*.

PAIR WORK

STUDENT B:
LOOK AT
PAGE 94

EXERCISE 1

You are a college student. *Student B* is your roommate. Ask *Student B* if you can:

Check (√) one:

Permission
given refused

wear *Student B's* new sweater on a date. ☐ ☐

watch a movie on TV tonight. ☐ ☐

use *Student B's* computer to do some homework. ☐ ☐

have a small party next Saturday night. ☐ ☐

use *Student B's* camera this weekend. ☐ ☐

invite a few friends over to play cards. ☐ ☐

borrow *Student B's* car Friday night. ☐ ☐

take *Student B's* pocket TV to the beach. ☐ ☐

EXERCISE 2

You are *Student B's* boss.
Student B is an office worker.
Look at the information in the box.
Answer *Student B's* requests.

Student B is a very good worker. You usually say "Yes" to *Student B's* requests, but remember these things:
- The company car can only be used for business.
- There's an important company meeting early Monday morning.
- This summer you want all the workers to take short vacations.

EXERCISE 3

You are a student. *Student B* is your teacher. Ask *Student B* for permission to:

Check (√) one:

Permission
given refused

borrow *Student B's* dictionary. ☐ ☐

leave class early today. ☐ ☐

hand in the book report one day late. ☐ ☐

come to class late tomorrow. ☐ ☐

change the subject of your history report. ☐ ☐

go to the rest room. ☐ ☐

take a make-up test for the exam you missed. ☐ ☐

miss class on Monday. ☐ ☐

EXERCISE 4

You are *Student B's* mother/father.
Student B is a teen-ager.
Look at the information in the box.
Answer *Student B's* requests.

Student B is a good son/daughter. You usually say "Yes" to *Student B's* requests, but remember these things:
- *Student B* has to study more after school and in the evening.
- You hate motorcycles—they're too dangerous.
- *Student B* is too young to go on a trip overseas with friends.

GROUP WORK

Choose *one* of the boxes below (pages 38~39).
Walk around the classroom and ask for permission
and give permission. Write the name of one person
next to each request.

○　Memo　○
• THE TEACHER MAY
  GIVE YOU A BOX.
• ALL OF THE BOXES ON
  ONE OR BOTH OF THE
  PAGES MUST BE USED.

1

Ask for permission to:

• borrow your friend's car. _____

• open a window. _____

• turn down the radio. _____

Give permission to:

• turn on the light.

• borrow your textbook.

• take your picture.

Refuse all other requests!

2

Ask for permission to:

• use your friend's computer. _____

• close the door. _____

• borrow your friend's textbook. _____

Give permission to:

• turn down the radio.

• use your telephone.

• borrow your sweater.

Refuse all other requests!

3

Ask for permission to:

• take your friend's picture. _____

• borrow your friend's sweater. _____

• turn off the TV. _____

Give permission to:

• use your computer.

• open a window.

• borrow your bicycle.

Refuse all other requests!

4

Ask for permission to:

• borrow your friend's bicycle. _____

• turn on the light. _____

• use your friend's telephone. _____

Give permission to:

• borrow your car.

• close the door.

• turn off the TV.

Refuse all other requests!

5

Ask for permission to:

• use your friend's surfboard. _____

• close a window. _____

• turn on the TV. _____

- -

Give permission to:

• play with your dog.

• borrow your skis.

• watch a movie on TV.

Refuse all other requests!

6

Ask for permission to:

• turn up the heat. _____

• read your friend's diary. _____

• borrow your friend's skis. _____

- -

Give permission to:

• turn on the TV.

• use your motorcycle.

• turn off the light.

Refuse all other requests!

7

Ask for permission to:

• watch a movie on TV. _____

• turn off the light. _____

• borrow your friend's boat. _____

- -

Give permission to:

• turn up the heat.

• close a window.

• open the door.

Refuse all other requests!

8

Ask for permission to:

• open the door. _____

• play with your friend's dog. _____

• use your friend's motorcycle._____

- -

Give permission to:

• use your surfboard.

• read your diary.

• borrow your boat.

Refuse all other requests!

HOMEWORK

Match the pictures with the dialogs and write a request for permission in each of the dialogs.

☐ **1** Rob: _____?

Deb: No, go right ahead, Rob.

Rob: Thanks. I'll open a window so it won't bother you.

Deb: No, that's okay—don't worry about it.

☐ **2** Tommy: _____?

Dad: Where to, Tommy?

Tommy: To my pen pal in Japan—just to say "Happy birthday."

Dad: Sure, go ahead. Just make sure you do it when it's the least expensive, okay?

☐ **3** René: _____?

Ali: Sure, René. You can use it all day if you like.

René: Thanks, but I just need it for now—I have one in my locker.

Ali: Oh, okay.

☐ **4** Harold: _____?

Sonny: Sunday? Where do you want to go?

Harold: I thought I would take Rebecca for a ride in the mountains.

Sonny: Well, okay—but be careful, Harold.

EXERCISE 2

Draw a simple sketch and write a short dialog with a request for permission and an answer.

7 EXCUSES, EXCUSES

PREVIEW

> **Why didn't you** <u>call me last night</u>**?**

> **I couldn't** <u>find your number</u>**.**
> **I had to** <u>take my brother to the airport</u>**.**
> **I** <u>forgot</u>**.**

1. Match the questions with the answers:

1. Why didn't you come home on time?
2. Why didn't you pick your sister up at school?
3. Why didn't you get a haircut?
4. Why didn't you send me a postcard?
5. Why didn't you do the homework?
6. Why didn't you watch that TV documentary for class?

☐ I couldn't find my textbook.
☐ I couldn't remember your address.
☐ I had to do homework all night.
☐ I had to work an extra hour.
☐ I didn't have any money.
☐ I lost my keys.

2. With a partner, make up a *different* excuse for each question above (1 through 6).

LISTENING TASK

EXERCISE 1

Listen to the conversation and circle Jonathan's excuses.

EXERCISE 2

Listen to the conversation again. Next to each of the excuses, make a "✔"if Mrs. Fenway believes the excuse, or an "**X**" if she doesn't believe it.

EXERCISE 3

After you listen to the conversation once more, look at the pictures and write down each of Jonathan's excuses as best as you can.

PAIR WORK

STUDENT B:
LOOK AT
PAGE 95

EXERCISE 1

You are a teacher. *Student B* is one of your students.
Ask *Student B* questions. Write down *Student B's* excuses.

Student B didn't...	*Student B's* excuse:
finish the test yesterday.	
come to class on Monday.	
bring any books to class today.	
come to class on time.	
finish writing the book report.	
do the homework.	

EXERCISE 2

You are a teen-ager. *Student B* is your mother/father.
Listen to each question and give *Student B* an excuse.
(Use the cues below.)

...find the vacuum cleaner.
...study for an English test.
...pick up the garbage can—it was too heavy!
...find the dog food.
... *(make up an excuse)*
... *(make up an excuse)*

EXERCISE 3

1. Write down a reason for each of the things you didn't do (1 through 6).
2. Walk around the classroom and ask for and give reasons for each (1 through 6).
    For at least three of your reasons, find someone who has a *similar* reason, and write down the name.

You didn't...	Your reason:	Name:
1. go bowling Friday night.		
2. go swimming on Saturday.		
3. go to the big party Saturday night.		
4. play ball Sunday morning.		
5. go shopping on Sunday.		
6. go to the movies Sunday night.		

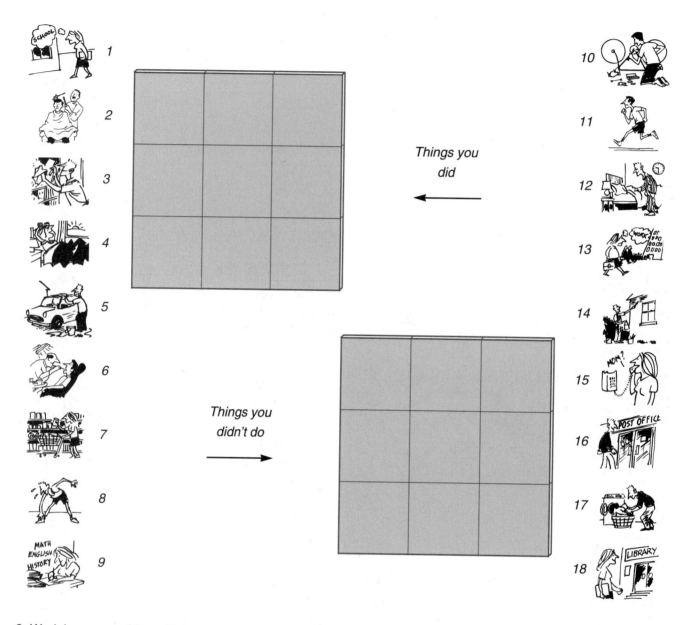

GROUP WORK

1. Look at the activities (1 through 18) and write the numbers in random order on your two grids.
(Do not show your grids to anyone.)

Things you did

←

Things you didn't do

→

2. Work in groups of four. Take turns asking each other about the activities (for example, *A* ask *B*, *B* ask *C*, etc.)
You must give a *reason* if you didn't do something. Circle any activity on your *"Things you did"* grid that
any other student did, and any activity on your *"Things you didn't do"* grid that any other student didn't do.
(Do not circle anything when *you* answer.)

The first player to get three circles in a straight line on <u>both</u> grids is the winner!

EXAMPLES:

STUDENT A: *"Did you go to school last Friday?"*
STUDENT B: *"Yes, I did."*

STUDENT B: *"Did you fix the bicycle yesterday?"*
STUDENT C: *"No, I didn't. I couldn't find the tools."*

○ Memo ○
• GIVE A <u>DIFFERENT</u>
  REASON EACH TIME
  YOU ANSWER "NO".
• WHEN IT'S YOUR TURN,
  YOU CAN ASK ANYONE
  IN YOUR GROUP.

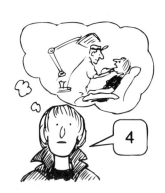

Look at the thoughts of each of the people that didn't go to Mike's party and write a reason for each person on a separate sheet of paper.

8 COULDN'T AGREE MORE

PREVIEW

In my opinion,	
I believe (that)	smoking cigarettes should not be allowed in public places.
I think (that)	

I don't think (that) smoking cigarettes should be allowed in public places.

I agree with you.	I don't agree with you.	
That's what I think.	I'm not sure that I agree.	Smokers have rights, too.
I think so too.	I don't think so.	
That's true.	That's true, but	
Absolutely.	Actually, I think (that)	smokers have rights, too.
I don't think so either.	*I disagree. I think (that)*	

Practice in groups of three: *Student A* give an <u>opinion</u>, *Student B* <u>agree</u>, and *Student C* <u>disagree and give a reason</u>.

<u>**Student A** (Opinion)</u>	<u>**Student B** (Agree)</u>	<u>**Student C** (Disagree / reason)</u>
1. ...watching television is a waste of time	...	...there are some <u>good</u> things on TV.
2. ...living and working in a big city is great.	...	...living in the country is much better.
3. ...police should give out more traffic tickets.	...	...the police give out too many <u>parking</u> tickets.
4. ...teachers assign too much homework.	...	...students need a lot of homework.
5. ...females are better at learning a foreign language.	...	...males learn foreign languages as well as females.

Change roles—*Student A, Student B,* and *Student C*—and practice again.

OPINION:	Bob	John	Sue	Mary
AGREE:				
DISAGREE:				

EXERCISE 1

Each picture shows an opinion.
Listen to the conversation and write
a number on each to show the order
that the opinions are given (1 through 3).

EXERCISE 2

Listen to the conversation again and
for each picture, circle the name of
the person who gives the opinion.

EXERCISE 3

Listen again and check (√) the names
of the people who agree or disagree
with each opinion.

OPINION:	Bob	John	Sue	Mary
AGREE:				
DISAGREE:				

OPINION:	Bob	John	Sue	Mary
AGREE:				
DISAGREE:				

PAIR WORK

ZOOS ARE CRUEL PLACES

THE GOVERNMENT SHOULD PROVIDE SHELTERS FOR HOMELESS PEOPLE

EVERYONE SHOULD LEARN AT LEAST TWO FOREIGN LANGUAGES

FAST FOOD RESTAURANTS SHOULD BE ABOLISHED

THERE'S TOO MUCH VIOLENCE ON TV

EXERCISE 1

1. Match the opinions above (pages 48~49) with the reasons below (page 48).

2. With a partner, take turns giving opinions and *agreeing*, using the opinions above and the reasons below.

EXAMPLE:
STUDENT *A:* *"I think zoos are cruel places."*
STUDENT *B:* *"That'ts true. Animals shouldn't be kept in cages."*

Animals shouldn't be kept in cages.

There's nothing to do, and there's no privacy.

It helps you to see your own country and culture more clearly.

It has a bad effect on young people.

The government should provide free education for everyone.

They are bad for the country's health.

It would help to improve international relations.

It's wrong to ignore them.

The air is dirty and there's too much noise.

You can buy things anytime, anywhere.

EXERCISE 2

1. Match the opinions above (pages 48~49) with the reasons below (page 49).

2. With a partner, take turns giving opinions and *disagreeing*, using the opinions above and the reasons below.

EXAMPLE:
STUDENT A: *"I think zoos are cruel places."*
STUDENT B: *"Actually, I think the animals are usually treated very well."*

The animals are usually treated very well.

You can learn just as much traveling around your *own* country.

Helping them find jobs and their own places to live is more important.

It's so difficult—I think learning *one* is enough.

They are not *all* terrible—some serve good food.

It's too easy to spend more than you have.

People are friendly and there's less crime.

It gives parents and students more choice.

They only put on what people want to watch.

There's so much to do—such as going to plays and the opera, and visiting museums and art galleries.

GROUP WORK

EXERCISE 1

Work in groups of three. Interview your partners
about the topics in your box on the right.
Take notes of the answers to your questions.

○ Memo ○
• DON'T JUST SAY
YOU LIKE OR DISLIKE
SOMETHING—
SAY WHY YOU LIKE IT
OR DON'T LIKE IT.

EXAMPLE:
STUDENT A: *"Keiko, what do you think about
watching sports on TV?"*
STUDENT B: *"I think it's a waste of time."*
STUDENT A: *"Do you agree, Juan?"*
STUDENT C: *"No, I think it's a great way to relax."*

Student A: Interview *Student B* and
Student C about the topics in this box:

~ *Watching sports on TV*
~ *Pro wrestling*
~ *Keeping pets*
~ *Traveling by bus*
~ *Learning to speak English*
~ *(Make up a topic!)*

Student B: Interview *Student A* and
Student C about the topics in this box:

~ *TV game shows*
~ *Health clubs*
~ *Loud parties*
~ *Traveling by train*
~ *Doing English homework*
~ *(Make up a topic!)*

Student C: Interview *Student A* and
Student B about the topics in this box:

~ *TV talk shows*
~ *Video games*
~ *Surprise parties*
~ *Traveling by plane*
~ *This group work exercise*
~ *(Make up a topic!)*

EXERCISE 2

The teacher may call on you to tell the class about your partners' opinions on one
of your topics. Look at your notes and tell the class what your partners said.

EXAMPLE:
TEACHER: *"Ivan, what do your partners think about watching sports on TV?"*
STUDENT A: *"Keiko thinks watching sports on TV is a waste of time, but Juan disagrees.
He thinks it's a great way to relax."*

HOMEWORK

For each statement of fact (A), give an opinion (B).
(Use *"should"* or *"shouldn't"* in your opinion.)
Then disagree with each opinion and give a reason (C).

Memo

• TRY TO USE DIFFERENT EXPRESSIONS IN YOUR OPINIONS AND WHEN YOU DISAGREE.

(A) Fact:	*(B) Opinion:*	*(C) Disagree / reason:*
Some teachers do not give homework.	I don't think that teachers should give homework.	I don't agree with you. In my opinion, homework is an important part of learning.
Some airlines only permit smoking on international flights.		
Some parks do not allow people to ride bicycles.		
Some apartment buildings do not rent to people with children.		
Some beaches prohibit people from playing music.		
Some taxis do not pick up people with pets.		
(Write your own statement)		

9 BIGGER AND BETTER

OH YEAH?

PREVIEW

The Mini	is smaller than	the Cadillac.
	is more economical than	
	isn't as comfortable as	

| Is the Mini | easier to park than | the Cadillac? | Yes, it is. |
| | as spacious as | | No, it isn't |

| Which is faster, the Mini or the Cadillac? | The Cadillac (is). |

Look at the pictures below. With a partner, talk about each one in the same way.

1

2

3

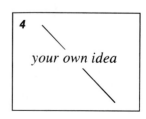
4

your own idea

LISTENING TASK

EXERCISE 1

Listen to the conversations (1 through 5) and check (√) the correct picture for each one.

1

2

3

4

5

EXERCISE 2

Listen again and write the number of each conversation (1 through 5) on any of the words that are used in comparisons.

( ) *long*   ( ) *delicious*   ( ) *nice*   ( ) *big*

( ) *comfortable*   ( ) *handsome*   ( ) *cheap*   ( ) *roomy*

( ) *sporty*   ( ) *good*   ( ) *mature*   ( ) *expensive*

EXERCISE 3

Listen once more and complete each of the following sentences using one of the words from *EXERCISE 2*. Then compare sentences with a partner.

1. *The white ones are* _____

2. *The red one is* _____

3. *The one on the right is* _____

4. *The Phuket tour is* _____

5. *The woman thinks hers is* _____

Student A:

Choose one of the collages below (pages 54~55), but don't tell *Student B* which one—*Student B* will ask you questions to find out which one.

Answer all questions with —"Yes" or "No."

car

movie

restaurant

BMW

EXAMPLE:

STUDENT B: "Is your car as expensive as a BMW?"

STUDENT A: "No, it's not."

○ Memo ○
• BEGIN ALL OF YOUR QUESTIONS WITH: "Is your car/movie/restaurant/chair/instrument/painting... ?"
• DON'T ASK: "Is it a Ford?"

chair

instrument

painting

Student B:

Find out which collage *Student A* has chosen by asking about comparison*s* between the small items (pages 54~55) and the large ones at the top.

Ask "yes/no" comparison questions only.

EXAMPLE:

STUDENT B: *"Is your movie more romantic than Star Wars?"*

STUDENT A: *"Yes, it is."*

○ Memo ○
• BOTH STUDENTS CAN CHOOSE COLLAGES AT THE SAME TIME AND TRY TO BE THE FIRST TO GUESS THE OTHER'S COLLAGE.

→ STUDENT A *and* STUDENT B: *Change roles and do the exercise again!*

GROUP WORK

EXERCISE 1

Look at the differences between the two pictures. Choose six differences and write a comparison for each on the lines below.

EXAMPLE:

"The yard was dirtier ten years ago."

○ Memo ○

• SOMETIMES USE "MORE/~ER _____" AND SOMETIMES USE "NOT AS _____".

EXERCISE 2

Go around the class and tell the others your comparisons and listen to theirs. For each of your comparisons, find someone who made a similar comparison and write his or her name on the right.

EXAMPLE:

"The yard is cleaner today."
"Right, the yard was dirtier ten years ago."

○ Memo ○

• IN LARGE CLASSES, FIND A DIFFERENT PERSON FOR EACH COMPARISON.

Comparison   *Student's Name*

_____   _____

_____   _____

_____   _____

_____   _____

_____   _____

_____   _____

HOMEWORK

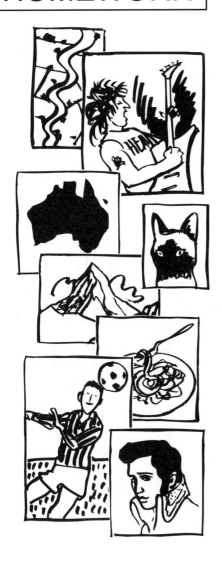

Write four opinion questions and four factual questions, comparing two things in each question.
See the box below for ideas, or use your own ideas.

TOPICS FOR COMPARISONS			
. animals	. cities	. countries	. famous people
. languages	. food	. music	. mountains
. oceans	. rivers	. sports	. TV programs

EXAMPLES:

(Opinion questions)

Which do you think is more interesting, rock music or jazz?
Do you think soccer is more exciting than baseball?

(Factual questions)

Is the Amazon River longer than the Mississippi River?
Which is larger, Australia or the United States?

○   Memo   ○
• ASK YOUR PARTNER
  YOUR QUESTIONS IN
  THE NEXT LESSON.
• MAKE SURE YOU KNOW
  THE ANSWER TO YOUR
  OWN FACTUAL QUESTIONS.

Questions

1. _____

2. _____

3. _____

4. _____

5. _____

6. _____

7. _____

8. _____

Student: Mrs. Lee, can I open a window?

Mrs. Lee: _____.

Wife: Is that you, dear? Did you pick up the groceries?

Husband: _____.

Husband: Why do you like the black one more than the white one?

Wife: _____

_____.

Don't you think so?

Husband: _____

_____.

LISTENING TASK

1. Listen to the conversations (1 through 5) and write the number of each conversation on the correct picture.

2. Listen again and write the *key words* next to each picture.

PAIR WORK

STUDENT B:
LOOK AT
PAGE 96

EXERCISE 1

Write a comparison for each picture (1 through 4):

Write a request for permission for each picture (5 through 8):

1 _____
_____

5 _____
_____

2 _____
_____

6 _____
_____

3 _____
_____

7 _____
_____

4 _____
_____

8 _____
_____

EXERCISE 2

Take turns with *Student B* guessing what each other wrote for each picture in *Exercise 1*.
These are *Student B's* pictures from *Exercise 1*:

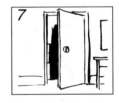

○ Memo ○
• EACH STUDENT
CAN MAKE ONLY
ONE GUESS PER TURN.
• THE WORDING DOES
NOT HAVE TO BE
EXACTLY THE SAME.

*The first one to guess all eight
correctly is the winner!*

60   UNIT 10

STUDENT B:
LOOK AT
PAGE 97

EXERCISE 3

1. Exchange the following opinions and responses with *Student B*, and write *Student B's* exact words on the correct lines below.

2. Discuss the topics with your partner, giving your *own* opinions.

○ Memo ○

• MATCH OPINIONS AND RESPONSES BY TALKING WITH STUDENT B — DO NOT READ EACH OTHER'S PAGES.

1 Student A: In my opinion, gambling should be illegal.
Student B: _____

2 Student B: _____
Student A: I don't think so. I think it's boring.

3 Student A: I think English is harder to learn than Chinese.
Student B: _____

4 Student B: _____
Student A: I'm not sure I agree. Most of them have very short careers.

5 Student A: I believe there's too much violence on TV.
Student B: _____

6 Student B: _____
Student A: I agree. I couldn't live without mine!

7 Student A: In my opinion, sightseeing tours are a waste of time—and they're so tiring!
Student B: _____

GROUP WORK

Make a circle of four (or more) students. Choose one student to begin. The first student must say why he didn't do something, using any picture below. The next student must repeat the statement and make one more similar statement using a different picture. Each student must repeat *every statement* and make one more statement.

Continue around the circle and use as many pictures as possible, repeating the statements in the same order—with names—until someone cannot repeat them all.

○ Memo ○

• HELP EACH OTHER REPEAT THE EXCUSES CORRECTLY.

EXAMPLE:

STUDENT 1: "I didn't exercise because I couldn't get up early."

(John)

STUDENT 2: "John didn't exercise because he couldn't get up early."
"I didn't wash the car because I had to study all day."

(Yuko)

STUDENT 3: "John didn't exercise because he couldn't get up early."
"Yuko didn't wash the car because she had to study all day."
"I didn't call because I didn't have the phone number."

(Vera)

The circle of students who use the most pictures—and correctly repeat the most excuses—are the winners!

LANGUAGE GAME

Play this game with two to six "players" and one "caller."

CALLER:
LOOK AT
PAGE 64

Take turns choosing two numbers (1 through 24) from the grid below.
Each number is a question or an answer. The caller will read each sentence that you choose.
Choose one number, listen to the caller read the sentence, and then choose another number.
Try to match a question with the answer. If you get a match, you get one extra turn (only) to choose again!

Do not write any notes—*just listen!*

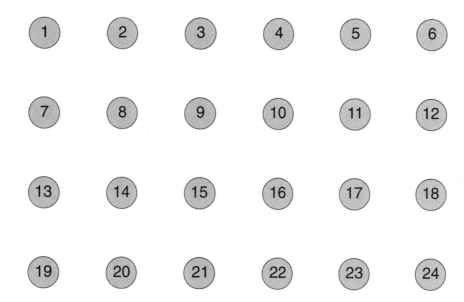

Continue until all the questions and answers have been matched.
The player with the most matches is the *winner!*

LANGUAGE GAME

PLAYERS:
LOOK AT
PAGE 63

Play this game with two to six "players" and one "caller."

1. Number the questions and answers below from 1 to 24 in *random order* (i.e., all mixed up).

2. The players will take turns choosing pairs of numbers.
Read aloud each of the two sentences that the player chooses, one at a time.
(The player will choose a second number <u>after</u> you read the first sentence.)
• If the two sentences *match,* shout "Match!" and write the player's name next to the sentences.
Then the same player gets one extra turn to choose two more numbers.
After that, the next player chooses.
• If the two sentences *do not match,* say "No match," and the next player chooses two numbers.

<u>Question:</u>	<u>Answer:</u>	<u>Player's name:</u>
◯ Can I use your calculator for a minute?	◯ Of course—it's on the table over there.	_____
◯ Why didn't you hand in the homework?	◯ I'm sorry, but my cat tore it up.	_____
◯ What do you think of life in New York?	◯ It can be dangerous, but I love it!	_____
◯ Is this house larger than yours?	◯ Actually, I think it's smaller.	_____
◯ Mind if I turn off the TV?	◯ Not at all—go ahead.	_____
◯ Why didn't you clean your room?	◯ Well, I couldn't find the vacuum cleaner.	_____
◯ The new mayor is great, isn't he?	◯ Actually, I'm not sure about him.	_____
◯ Is the Nile longer than the Mississippi?	◯ Sure, it's about 1800 miles longer.	_____
◯ Could I possibly use your car tonight?	◯ I'm sorry, but it has two flat tires.	_____
◯ Why weren't you at my surprise party?	◯ I wasn't invited!	_____
◯ I think TV is bad for children, don't you?	◯ Well, I think that too much can be harmful.	_____
◯ Is your dog friendlier than your cat?	◯ Yeah, but my cat is smarter.	_____

Continue until all the questions and answers are matched.
The player with the most matches is the *winner!*

○ Memo ○

• READ EACH SENTENCE
SLOWLY, NO MORE
THAN TWO TIMES.
• PLAYERS MUST
NOT LOOK AT THIS PAGE.

UNIT 10

11 IF I WERE YOU

PREVIEW

What's	the matter? wrong?

I have a <u>toothache</u>.

You should You ought to You'd better Why don't you If I were you, I'd	<u>go to the dentist</u>.

Right, maybe I will.
I think I will.
I guess I should.
Yeah, that's a good idea.
Yes, I'm going to.

1. Match the problems with the advice:

1. I have a high fever and a bad headache.
2. I've been working overtime until midnight all week.
3. I think my car battery is almost dead.
4. Someone stole my checkbook!
5. Somebody hit my car in the middle of the night.

☐ You should call the bank immediately.
☐ You ought to buy a new one.
☐ You'd better call the police.
☐ Why don't you take a break?
☐ If I were you, I'd see a doctor.

2. With a partner, make up *different* advice for each problem above (1 through 5).

LISTENING TASK

EXERCISE 1

Listen to the conversation and circle the things that are suggested to Elizabeth.

EXERCISE 2

Listen to the conversation again.
Next to each of the suggestions, write
a "✔" if Elizabeth accepts the idea,
a "?" if she *may* accept the idea, or
an "X" if she rejects the idea.

PAIR WORK

STUDENT B:
LOOK AT
PAGE 98

EXERCISE 1

Ask *Student B:* "What's wrong?" *or* "What's the matter?"
Listen and give *Student B* advice.
(Choose the best advice from the cues on the right.)

...the bank

...a doctor

...the police

...study very hard

...the restaurant

...some aspirin

...(make up your own advice!)

EXERCISE 2

Tell *Student B* your problems (1 through 7).
Write down *Student B's* advice for each.

1. You left your camera on the train.

_____

2. You only slept two hours last night.

_____

3. You lost your passport.

_____

4. You have a cold and a sore throat.

_____

5. You locked your keys in your car.

_____

6. You have a toothache.

_____

7. *(make up a problem)*

_____

EXERCISE 3

Student B is taking a trip to Hong Kong.
Listen to the plans and give *Student B* advice.
(Choose the best advice from the cues below.)

EXAMPLE:
STUDENT B: "I'm going to stay at the Excelsior Hotel.
           Do you think that's a good idea?"
STUDENT A: "Why don't you stay at the YMCA?
           It's much cheaper."

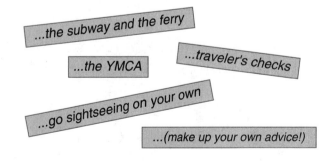

...the subway and the ferry

...the YMCA

...traveler's checks

...go sightseeing on your own

...(make up your own advice!)

EXERCISE 4

1. *Student B* will tell you the name of a place that *Student B* knows well.

2. Tell *Student B* that you are going to take a trip to this place on vacation next summer.
Listen to *Student B's* advice and write it down.

→ STUDENT A and STUDENT B: Change roles and do Exercise 4 again!

GROUP WORK

EXERCISE 1

Write down some advice for each person (1 through 5) below each picture.

EXERCISE 2

Walk around the classroom and ask for advice or give advice for each of the problems.
Next to each problem, write the name of anyone with advice *similar* to yours.

1

* or "boyfriend"

_____

_____

_____

2

_____

_____

_____

3

_____

_____

_____

4

_____

_____

_____

5

_____

_____

_____

HOMEWORK

EXERCISE 1

Look at the pictures and write a suggestion in each dialog.
(Use *"We should…"*, *"We ought to…"*, or *"Why don't we…?"* for the suggestions.)

Husband: It's our first wedding anniversary next month, honey! What shall we do to celebrate?

Wife: _____

Husband: Well, it'll be expensive, but... Sure! Let's go!

Husband: Our third anniversary is just two weeks away! What do you think we should do?

Wife: _____

Husband: That's a great idea! We can invite everyone!

Wife: Next week's our fifth anniversary. What do you want to do?

Husband: _____

Wife: Sure, that sounds nice—just the two of us.

Wife: It's our tenth anniversary this Friday. You want to do anything?

Husband: _____

Wife: Yeah, okay—we haven't been out in a while.

Wife: Today's our twentieth anniversary... John? John!

Husband: _____

Wife: Okay. Is there anything good on?

EXERCISE 2

Draw a simple sketch in the thought balloon and write the rest of the dialog.

Wife: Yesterday was our fiftieth anniversary, John. Let's do something.

Husband: _____

Wife: _____

PREVIEW

1. Practice the following dialogs with a partner.

Student A:	**Have you ever done any bungy-jumping?**
Student B	**Yes, I have. I did some last year.**
Student A:	**What was it like?**
Student B:	**It was fantastic! How about you?**
Student A:	**No, never.**

Student A:	**Have you ever been to Europe?**
Student B	**No, I haven't. Have you?**
Student A:	**Yes, I've been there a few times.**
Student B:	**When did you last go there?**
Student A:	**I went two years ago—I had a great time.**

2. Have similar dialogs about yourselves, using these ideas:

Your own idea (sports activity)

Your own idea (travel)

LISTENING TASK

1. Look at the pictures, and then listen to the conversation with your book closed.

2. Open you book and number the pictures in the correct order, according to Linda's story.

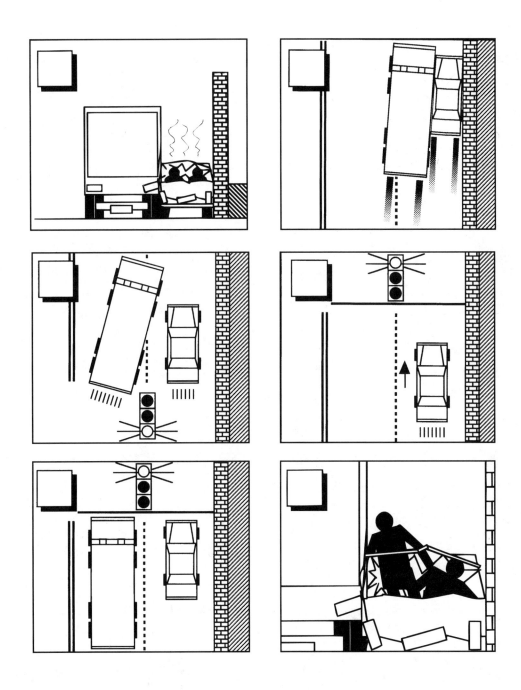

3. Listen again and write the *key words* next to each picture.

PAIR WORK

○ Memo ○
• DO NOT READ
THE SENTENCES
TO STUDENT B:
JUST ANSWER
THE QUESTIONS!

STUDENT B:
LOOK AT
PAGE 99

Take turns with *Student B* asking and answering questions about the people below. For the empty boxes, find out:

• *where* they have been (ask about places in the box below)
• *when* they went there
• *why* they went

PLACES
• Hong Kong • Tokyo
• Senegal • Nepal
• Moscow • Cairo

First write notes of the answers *next* to each empty box, and later write one sentence with all the information *in* each box.

(Afterwards compare all your sentences with Student B's sentences.)

KATRINA

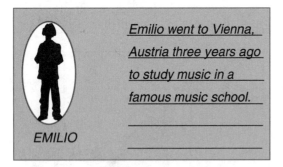

KURT

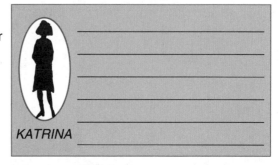

JIM

Last year Jim flew to Australia with some friends to take part in a surfing competition.

EMILIO

Emilio went to Vienna, Austria three years ago to study music in a famous music school.

JACK & ERI

STUDENT B

DEBBIE & TOM

Debbie and Tom drove from New York City to Aspen, Colorado to go skiing in January.

GROUP WORK

EXERCISE 1

1. Choose three of the topics below and write a *"Have you ever ~ ?"* question for each one.

2. Ask around the class and—for each question— find someone who answers "Yes" and write down his or her name. Then ask a few more questions about the experience and write down the details (when, where, why, etc.).

TOPICS
- a strange experience
- a movie
- music
- a job
- language learning
- losing something
- foreign travel
- your own idea

○   Memo   ○
- MAKE SURE EACH QUESTION IS SPECIFIC!
- YOU SHOULD SPEAK TO THREE DIFFERENT PEOPLE.

Topic:
Question:

Name:
Details:

Topic:
Question:

Name:
Details:

Topic:
Question:

Name:
Details:

EXERCISE 2

The teacher may call on you to tell the class about one of the experiences you've asked about.
Look at your notes on the details for the experience and tell the class the story.

HOMEWORK

Write a *"Have you ever ~ ?"* question for each of the pictures.

Use one of the ideas above, and write a conversation between you and a friend.
Your experience can be true *or* imaginary.

Friend: Have you ever _____ ?

You: Yes, I have, actually.

Friend: _____

You: _____

Friend: _____

You: _____

_____

_____

_____

_____

13 **HOW ABOUT DINNER?**

PREVIEW

Would you like to	go to a movie tonight?
How about Do you feel like	going to the beach tomorrow?

I'd love to.	I'd love to, but	
That sounds <u>great</u>.	That sounds great, but	I have to study for a test.
That's a <u>great</u> idea!	I'm sorry, but	

With a partner, practice inviting each other and accepting or refusing invitations.
Look at the pictures below for ideas.

EXERCISE 1

Circle all the things that Zachary invites Mia to do,
and check (√) the one that she says "Yes" to.

EXERCISE 2

Draw a square around each reason that Mia gives Zachary when she says "No,"
and match each reason with the correct invitation.

PAIR WORK

1. Choose sixteen of the activities and write the numbers in random order on your grid.
   (Do not show the grid to your partner.)

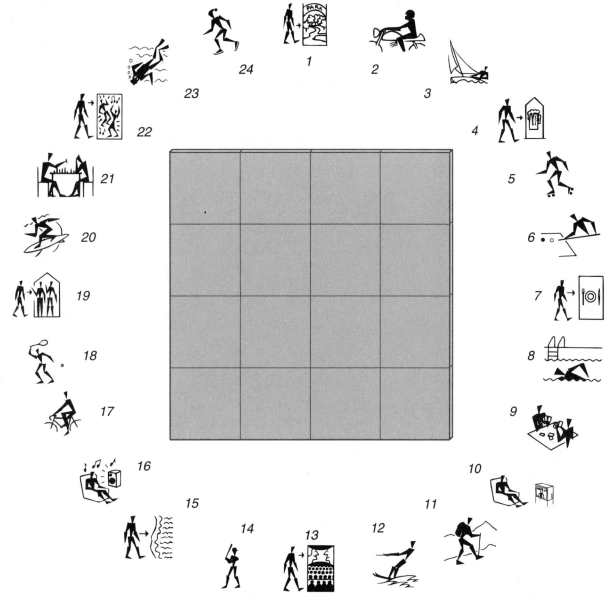

2. With a partner, take turns inviting each other to do the activities on your grid. *You can accept or refuse any invitation.* You must give a *reason* if you refuse. Circle (**O**) the activity on your grid if your partner accepts the invitation. Cross off (**X**) the activity on your grid if your partner refuses the invitation. (Do not circle or cross off anything when *you* answer.)

   The first player to get either four **O**'s or four **X**'s in a straight line is the winner!

EXAMPLES:

STUDENT A: *"Would you like to go to the park tomorrow?"*
STUDENT B: *"Sure, I'd love to."*

STUDENT B: *"How about playing tennis on Saturday?"*
STUDENT A: *"I'm sorry, but I have to work."*

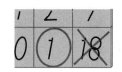

> o   Memo   o
> • GIVE A DIFFERENT REASON EACH TIME YOU REFUSE AN INVITATION.
> • MAKE ANOTHER GRID WHEN YOU'RE FINISHED AND PLAY AGAIN.

GROUP WORK

1. Fill in any five mornings, five afternoons, and five evenings on the schedule below with different activities—things that you have to do or dates that you have.

(Choose from the activities on the right, or make up your own.)

	MONDAY	TUESDAY	WEDNESDAY	THURSDAY	FRIDAY	SATURDAY	SUNDAY
MORNING							
AFTERNOON							
EVENING							

2. Walk around the classroom and make dates with four different people:
- one person in the morning
- one person in the afternoon
- one person in the evening
- one person anytime

You can only make a date for a time you are free.

For each date, write on the schedule:
- who you will meet
- the activity (choose from the left, or make up your own)
- when you will meet
- where you will meet

EXAMPLE:

STUDENT A: *"Would you like to go to a movie Friday night?"*
STUDENT B: *"I'm sorry, but I have to work."*
STUDENT A: *"Then how about Saturday night?"*
STUDENT B: *"Sure, that sounds great."*
STUDENT A: *"Okay, how about meeting at my house around six?"*
STUDENT B: *"Sure, that's fine."*

○ Memo ○
- GIVE A REASON EACH TIME YOU REFUSE AN INVITATION.
- IF SOMEONE REFUSES YOUR INVITATION, SUGGEST ANOTHER TIME.

UNIT 13

HOMEWORK

Write the lines of this dialog *in order* on the lines below.

That sounds great — where shall we meet?

Well, listen, Rob, would you like to go to a movie Sunday night?

How about meeting at the mall around six o'clock?

Oh, then how about Saturday night?

Diane, how about going to a movie on Saturday afternoon?

Sure, six o'clock is fine.

I'm sorry, but Saturday night I'm going to a concert with Sue.

A concert? Oh, well, then maybe another time...

I'd love to, but I have to work in the afternoon.

That's a great idea.

Good. How about seeing "*Jurassic Park Revisited?*"

1. Rob: _____

2. Diane: I'd love to, but I have to work in the afternoon. _____

3. Rob: _____

4. Diane: _____

5. Rob: _____

6. Diane: _____

7. Rob: That's a great idea. _____

8. Diane: _____

9. Rob: _____

10. Diane: How about meeting at the mall around six o'clock? ____

11. Rob: _____

PREVIEW

I'm sure they'll <u>win.</u>

They're definitely going to <u>win.</u>

They'll <u>win.</u>

They're going to <u>win.</u>

I think they'll <u>win.</u>

They'll probably <u>win.</u>

Maybe they'll <u>win.</u>

They *could* <u>win.</u>

They might <u>win.</u>

1. Match the lines in column A with the lines in column B:

A	B
1. Look at those clouds!	☐ No, I think they'll go down.
2. Do you think rents will go up next year?	☐ It could be in the stores early next year.
3. Is the factory going to close down?	☐ I'm not so sure. Maybe he will.
4. She could be head teacher someday.	☐ It might. It depends on profits.
5. He's definitely going to win the election.	☐ Oh, I'm sure she will.
6. When will their new album be out?	☐ Yeah, it's going to pour.

2. Look at the pictures (1 through 6). Practice short exchanges like the ones above with a partner.

English test

Job application

Weather forecast

Dollar foreign exchange rate

College

(Your own idea)

LISTENING TASK

EXERCISE 1

Listen to the conversation and circle the pictures that best represent the predictions that you hear.

EXERCISE 2

Listen to the conversation again. Next to each of the predictions, write a "✔" if the person is certain, and a "?" if the person isn't sure.

EXERCISE 3

Listen once more and note the exact wording of each prediction. Then go over each prediction with a partner.

Student A:

Look at each question on page 83 and make a prediction about *Student B's* future.

Check (√) "*Agrees*" if *Student B* agrees, or "*Disagrees*" if *Student B* disagrees.

Student B:

Listen to *Student A's* predictions and tell *Student A* if you agree or disagree.

	Agrees	Disagrees

EXAMPLES:

STUDENT A: "I think you will definitely be a student at this school next year." ☑ ☐
STUDENT B: "You're right, I will."

STUDENT A: "I think you might be a student. at this school next year." ☐ ☑
STUDENT B: "No, I don't think so."

STUDENT A: "I don't think you'll be a student. at this school next year." ☑ ☐
STUDENT B: "I don't think so either."

Do you think your partner will...

Memo

• STUDENT B:
CLOSE YOUR BOOK
DURING THE EXERCISE
AND ANSWER
TRUTHFULLY!

	Agrees	Disagrees
...be a student at this school next year?	☐	☐
...study another foreign language besides English someday?	☐	☐
...go overseas to study someday?	☐	☐
...change jobs some time during the next five years?	☐	☐
...be living in the same place two years from now?	☐	☐
...buy a car this year?	☐	☐
...buy a house some time during the next ten years?	☐	☐
...have grandchildren someday?	☐	☐
...go abroad on vacation in the next few years?	☐	☐
...live in another country some time in the future?	☐	☐
...be famous someday?	☐	☐
...(Write and ask your own question:) _____?	☐	☐
Total:	_____	_____

→ *STUDENT A and STUDENT B: Change roles and do the exercise again!*

GROUP WORK

Good evening, everyone. This is Dan Fairly with focus on America. Our topic for tonight is life in the future. We went out into the streets today and asked people for their predictions. Connie?

Thanks, Dan. I asked ten people this question: "Do you think the world will be a better place in fifty years?" Well, seven people said "No," and only three people said "Yes." Giselle?

Thanks, Connie. I asked ten people this question: "Do you think…"

1. Work in groups of three or four. You are a team of TV news reporters. You are going to ask the other students in the class about life in the future. Work out a different "yes/no" question for each member of your group, and write your own question below. (See the *topic box* for things to ask about.)

_____

_____

_____

TOPIC BOX

- *the environment*
- *space travel*
- *transportation*
- *shopping*
- *homes*
- *computers*
- *clothes*
- *schools*
- *offices*
- *(your own idea)*

2. Go around the classroom and put your question to as many people as you can. Put one check (√) in the correct box below for each response ("Yes" or "No").

YES	*NO*

3. With the other members in your group, present the results of your survey to the class. (You can use the language at the top of the page as a model.)

HOMEWORK

Make six predictions about the future.

1. _____

   _____

2. _____

   _____

3. _____

   _____

4. _____

   _____

5. _____

   _____

6. _____

   _____

○ Memo ○

• AFTERWARDS, SEE IF YOU AGREE WITH YOUR CLASS- MATES' PREDICTIONS.

15 SAY THAT AGAIN

Work with a partner and write a dialog to go with the picture story.

LISTENING TASK

1. Listen to the conversations (1 through 5) and write the number
of each conversation on the correct picture.

2. Listen again and write the *key words* next to each picture.

PAIR WORK

STUDENT B:
LOOK AT
PAGE 100

EXERCISE 1

Give *Student B* clues for each answer in *CROSSWORD PUZZLE 1*
until *Student B* guesses the answer. Use "blanks" in your clues.

EXAMPLE:
STUDENT B: "What's 1 down?"
STUDENT A: "I BLANK with you—I don't think cats are smarter
             than dogs."
STUDENT B: "Disagree?"
STUDENT A: "That's right!"

For help making clues, look at the *Preview* section of the unit
shown for each word, but try to make up your own sentences.

CROSSWORD PUZZLE 1

Unit 8   Warm-up   Unit 12   Unit 6   Unit 8 / Unit 13

Unit 9

Unit 4

Unit 7

Unit 13

UNIT 4 - INSTRUCTIONS
UNIT 13 - INVITING
UNIT 7 - EXCUSES & REASONS
UNIT 12 - EXPERIENCES
WARM-UP - PERSONAL INFORMATION
UNIT 8 - OPINIONS
UNIT 9 - COMPARISONS
UNIT 6 - PERMISSION

EXERCISE 2

Ask *Student B* for clues and fill in *CROSSWORD PUZZLE 2*.
In each clue, the "blank" in *Student B's* sentence is the answer.

EXAMPLE:
STUDENT A: "What's 1 down?"
STUDENT B: "He's poor now, but I'm sure he'll be rich BLANK."
STUDENT A: "Someday?"
STUDENT B: "That's right!"

CROSSWORD PUZZLE

○ Memo ○
• ONLY THE STUDENT
  GIVING CLUES SHOULD
  LOOK BACK AT THE UNITS.
• YOU CAN GIVE MORE
  THAN ONE CLUE FOR
  EACH ANSWER.

UNIT 15

GROUP WORK

Work in groups of four.

Student A:

Tell the group a story about yourself. *The story must be 100% true or 100% false.* Don't tell the other students in your group if it is true or false—they will ask you questions about your story, and then tell you whether they think it is true or false.

Students B, C, & D:

Listen to *Student A's* story and then ask questions about the story. Afterwards tell *Student A* whether you think the story is true or false.

After all the stories, vote for the "best lie" and the "most unbelievable true story."

Memo

• EACH STUDENT TAKE
A TURN AS STUDENT A
AND
TELL THE GROUP A STORY.

LANGUAGE GAME

CALLER:
LOOK AT
PAGE 91

Play this game in class with two to four "players" and one "caller."

Take turns choosing two numbers (1 through 20) from the grid below.
Each number is a question or an answer. The caller will read each sentence that you choose.
Choose one number, listen to the caller read the sentence, and then choose another number.
Try to match a question with the answer. If you get a match, you get one extra turn (only) to choose again!

Do not write any notes—*just listen!*

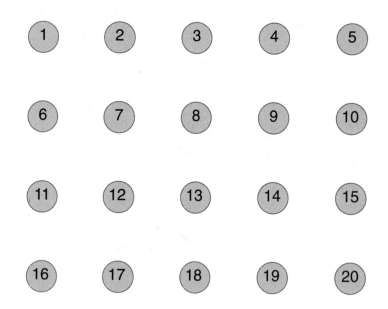

Continue until all the questions and answers have been matched.
The player with the most matches is the *winner!*

○ Memo ○

• CHECK (√) THE NUMBERS
THAT YOU MATCH.
• CROSS OFF (X) THE
NUMBERS THAT
ANOTHER PLAYER MATCHES.

LANGUAGE GAME

PLAYERS:
LOOK AT
PAGE 90

EXERCISE 1

Look through the book for ideas and write ten questions and answers side by side in the blanks below.
Then number the questions and answers from 1 to 20 in *random order* (i.e., all mixed up).

EXERCISE 2

Play this game with two to four "players" and one "caller."

The players will take turns choosing pairs of numbers.
Read aloud each of the two sentences that the player chooses, one at a time.
(The player will choose a second number <u>after</u> you read the first sentence.)
- If the two sentences *match,* shout "Match!" and write the player's name next to the sentences.
  Then the same player gets one extra turn to choose two more numbers.
  After that, the next player chooses.
- If the two sentences *do not match,* say "No match," and the next player chooses two numbers.

Question:	*Answer:*	*Player's name:*
◯ ———————	◯ ———————	———————
◯ ———————	◯ ———————	———————
◯ ———————	◯ ———————	———————
◯ ———————	◯ ———————	———————
◯ ———————	◯ ———————	———————
◯ ———————	◯ ———————	———————
◯ ———————	◯ ———————	———————
◯ ———————	◯ ———————	———————
◯ ———————	◯ ———————	———————
◯ ———————	◯ ———————	———————

Continue until all the questions and answers are matched.
The player with the most matches is the *winner!*

◯ Memo ◯

• IMPORTANT:
MAKE SURE THAT EACH
ANSWER CANNOT BE USED
WITH ANY OTHER QUESTION.
• THE TEACHER MAY CHECK
YOUR SENTENCES.

WARM-UP UNIT   STUDENT B

STUDENT A:
LOOK AT
PAGE 4

1. Take turns with *Student A* asking and answering questions, and fill in the blanks in the three paragraphs below (1 through 3).

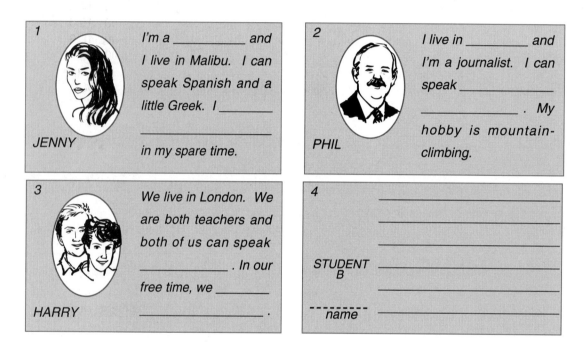

1

JENNY

I'm a _____ and I live in Malibu. I can speak Spanish and a little Greek. I _____ _____ in my spare time.

2

PHIL

I live in _____ and I'm a journalist. I can speak _____ _____ . My hobby is mountain-climbing.

3

HARRY

We live in London. We are both teachers and both of us can speak _____ . In our free time, we _____ _____ .

4

STUDENT B

- - - - - - - -
name

_____
_____
_____
_____
_____
_____

2. Take turns with *Student A* asking and answering questions, and write a short paragraph like the others about *Student A* in box number 4.

PAIR WORK

STUDENT B

STUDENT A:
LOOK AT
PAGE 7

EXERCISE 1

You work at the Port Authority Bus Terminal.
Look at the bus schedule and
answer *Student A's* questions.

PORT AUTHORITY BUS TERMINAL				
BUS INFORMATION				
DESTINATION:	*MIAMI*		*DENVER*	
FARE:	*$102*		*$119*	
	Departs	Arrives	Departs	Arrives
	6:00	6:15	6:15	4:45
DAILY	8:30	8:45	8:40	7:10
DEPARTURE	10:40	10:55	10:50	9:20
AND	13:30	13:45	13:40	12:10
ARRIVAL	15:30	15:45	15:30	14:00
TIMES:	16:30	16:45	17:00	15:30
	17:45	18:00	18:00	16:30
	19:00	19:15	22:00	20:30
ARRIVAL DAY:	*+ one day*		*+ two days*	
TRAVEL TIME:	*24 hrs. 15 min.*		*48 hrs. 30 min.*	

EXERCISE 2

You are going to take a train trip from New York City to another city.
Choose *where* you want to go and *when* you want to leave:

You want to go to ❏ *Chicago.*
                     ❏ *Los Angeles.*

You want to leave on ❏ *Monday,*
                      ❏ *Thursday,*
                      ❏ *Friday,*

   at about ___*o'clock*

   in the ❏ *morning.*
               ❏ *afternoon.*
               ❏ *evening.*

NOTES

How Much?

When leave?

When arrive?

How long?

Student A works at New York Penn Station.
Ask *Student A* questions and write the answers In the notebook.

EXERCISE 3

You want to take a language course this summer.
Student A is a language school manager.
Choose a language to study and ask *Student A* questions.
(See the box below for ideas.)
Make a note of your questions and the answers.

EXAMPLE:
STUDENT B: *"Could you tell me if you have a Chinese course?"*
STUDENT A: *"Yes, we do."*

POSSIBLE THINGS TO ASK ABOUT		
• _____ language	• *Course dates*	• *Class times*
• *Placement test*	• *Length of course*	• *Students*
• *Teachers*	• *Costs*	• *School location*

→ **STUDENT A** and **STUDENT B:**
Change roles and do Exercise 3 again!

PAIR WORK

UNIT 6

STUDENT B

STUDENT A:
LOOK AT
PAGE 37

EXERCISE 1

You are a college student.
Student A is your roommate.
Look at the information in the box.
Answer *Student A's* requests.

Student A is a great roommate. You usually say "Yes" to
Student A's requests, but remember these things:
- You are going to take a friend to a drive-in movie Friday night.
- You have to watch a documentary on TV tonight for history class.
- You are going to take pictures at a friend's wedding on Sunday.

EXERCISE 2

You are an office worker. *Student A* is your boss.
Ask *Student A* for permission to:

Check (√) one:

Permission
given   refused

take a thirty-minute break to go to the bank.   ☐   ☐

take this Friday off.   ☐   ☐

come to work late on Monday.   ☐   ☐

take a two-hour lunch break tomorrow.   ☐   ☐

make a personal overseas phone call.   ☐   ☐

use the company car over the weekend.   ☐   ☐

get a new telephone.   ☐   ☐

take a four-week vacation this summer.   ☐   ☐

EXERCISE 3

You are a teacher.
Student A is your student
Look at the information in the box.
Answer *Student A's* requests.

Student A is a good student. You usually say "Yes" to
Student A's requests, but remember these things:
- You do not like it when students come to class late.
- You do not let students leave early unless it's an emergency.
- You do not want *Student A* to miss any classes.

EXERCISE 4

You are a teen-ager. *Student A* is your parent
(mother/father). Ask *Student A* if you can:

Check (√) one:

Permission
given refused

invite a friend to dinner.   ☐   ☐

get a part-time job in the evening.   ☐   ☐

go on a camping trip with friends.   ☐   ☐

buy a small motorcycle.   ☐   ☐

sleep at a friend's house this weekend.   ☐   ☐

paint your bedroom black and white.   ☐   ☐

have a party next weekend.   ☐   ☐

go to France for the summer with friends.   ☐   ☐

PAIR WORK

STUDENT B

STUDENT A:
LOOK AT
PAGE 43

EXERCISE 1

You are a student. *Student A* is your teacher.
Listen to each question and give *Student A* an excuse.
(Use the cues below.)

...remember the answers.

...visit my aunt in the hospital.

...open my locker.

...go to the dentist this morning.

... *(make up an excuse)*

... *(make up an excuse)*

EXERCISE 2

You are *Student A's* mother/father. *Student A* is a teen-ager.
Ask *Student A* questions. Write down *Student A's* excuses.

Student A didn't...	*Student A's* excuse:
clean the basement.	_____
do the laundry.	_____
take out the garbage.	_____
feed the dog.	_____
wash the dishes.	_____
get a haircut.	_____

EXERCISE 3

1. Write down a reason for each of the things you didn't do (1 through 6).

2. Walk around the classroom and ask for and give reasons for each (1 through 6).
   For at least three of your reasons, find someone who has a *similar* reason, and write down the name.

You didn't...	Your reason:	Name:
1. go bowling Friday night.	_____	_____
2. go swimming on Saturday.	_____	_____
3. go to the big party Saturday night.	_____	_____
4. play ball Sunday morning.	_____	_____
5. go shopping on Sunday.	_____	_____
6. go to the movies Sunday night.	_____	_____

EXERCISE 1

Write a comparison for each picture (1 through 4):   Write a request for permission for each picture (5 through 8):

1  _____
  _____

5  _____

2  _____
  _____

6  _____

3  _____
  _____

7  _____

4  _____
  _____

8  _____

EXERCISE 2

Take turns with *Student A* guessing what each other wrote for each picture in *Exercise 1*.
These are *Student A's* pictures from *Exercise 1*:

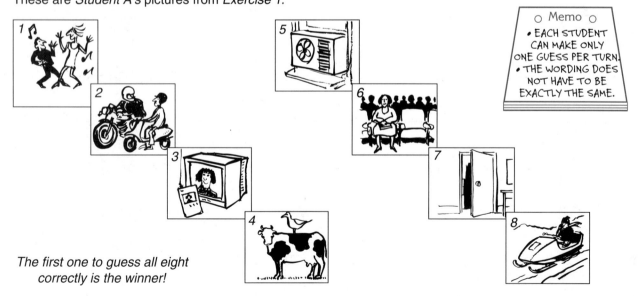

○ Memo ○
• EACH STUDENT
CAN MAKE ONLY
ONE GUESS PER TURN.
• THE WORDING DOES
NOT HAVE TO BE
EXACTLY THE SAME.

*The first one to guess all eight
correctly is the winner!*

PAIR WORK

UNIT 10

STUDENT B

STUDENT A:
LOOK AT
PAGE 61

EXERCISE 3

1. Exchange the following opinions and responses with *Student A*, and write *Student A's* exact words on the correct lines below.

2. Discuss the topics with your partner, giving your *own* opinions.

○ Memo ○
• MATCH OPINIONS
AND RESPONSES BY
TALKING WITH
STUDENT A —
DO NOT READ
EACH OTHER'S PAGES.

1 Student A: _____

   Student B: *Absolutely. I like to stay in one place and relax.*

2 Student B: *In my opinion, a computer is a real necessity these days.*

   Student A: _____

3 Student A: _____

   Student B: *That's what I think. Last night I saw six murders in one hour!*

4 Student B: *I think professional athletes are highly overpaid.*

   Student A: _____

5 Student A: _____

   Student B: *I think so, too. Some people lose their life savings!*

6 Student B: *I think this exercise is really interesting, don't you?*

   Student A: _____

7 Student A: _____

   Student B: *Actually, I think Chinese is the hardest language to learn in the world.*

PAIR WORK

STUDENT A:
LOOK AT
PAGE 67

EXERCISE 1

Tell *Student A* your problems (1 through 7).
Write down *Student A's* advice for each.

1. You have a headache.

_____

2. You have a big test next Monday.

_____

3. You lost your cash card.

_____

4. You have stomach pains and a fever.

_____

5. Someone stole your bicycle!

_____

6. You left your wallet at a restaurant.

_____

7. (*make up a problem*)

_____

EXERCISE 2

Ask *Student A:* "What's wrong?" *or* "What's the matter?"
Listen and give *Student A* advice.
(Choose the best advice from the cues below.)

...the "Lost and found" office

...medicine

...the dentist

...go to sleep early tonight

...a locksmith

...the embassy

...(make up your own advice!)

EXERCISE 3

You are taking a trip to Hong Kong.
Tell *Student A* your plans (1 through 5).
Ask *Student A* for advice and write it down.

EXAMPLE:
STUDENT B: "I'm going to stay at the Excelsior Hotel.
Do you think that's a good idea?"
STUDENT A: "Why don't you stay at the YMCA?
It's much cheaper."

1. ...stay at the Excelsior Hotel.

_____

2. ...travel around Hong Kong by taxi.

_____

3. ...take cash.

_____

4. ...go on a few sightseeing tours.

_____

5. ... (*make up a plan*)

_____

EXERCISE 4

1. Tell *Student A* the name of the place that you know well.

2. Give *Student A* advice about where to stay, what to see, how to get around, and so on.

→ **STUDENT A** and **STUDENT B:** Change roles and do Exercise 4 again!

PAIR WORK

Take turns with *Student A* asking and answering questions about the people below. For the empty boxes, find out:

- *where* they have been (ask about places in the box below)
- *when* they went there
- *why* they went

○ Memo ○
- DO NOT READ THE SENTENCES TO STUDENT A: JUST ANSWER THE QUESTIONS!

STUDENT A: LOOK AT PAGE 72

PLACES
- Colorado
- Florida
- Australia
- Vienna
- Spain
- Israel

First write notes of the answers *next* to each empty box, and later write one sentence with all the information *in* each box.

(Afterwards compare all your sentences with Student A's sentences.)

JIM
_____
_____
_____
_____
_____

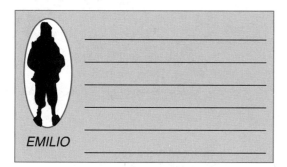

EMILIO
_____
_____
_____
_____
_____

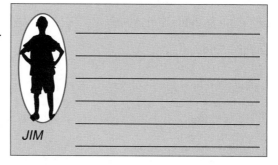

KATRINA
Ten years ago Katrina flew to Moscow to visit her brother, and she met her brother's wife and children for the first time.

KURT
Kurt went to Nepal to go trekking on Mount Everest last October, and spent three weeks in the mountains.

DEBBIE & TOM
_____
_____
_____
_____
_____

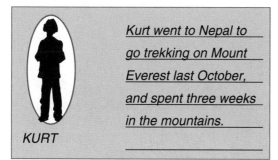

STUDENT A
_____
_____
_____
_____
_____

JACK & ERI
During the winter vacation Jack and Eri travelled to Hong Kong to go shopping, and they spent a lot of money.

STUDENT A:
LOOK AT
PAGE 88

EXERCISE 1

Ask *Student A* for clues and fill in *CROSSWORD PUZZLE 1*.
In each clue, the "blank" in *Student A's* sentence is the answer.

EXAMPLE:
STUDENT B: "What's 1 down?"
STUDENT A: "I BLANK with you—I don't think cats are smarter than dogs."
STUDENT B: "Disagree?"
STUDENT A: "That's right!"

CROSSWORD PUZZLE

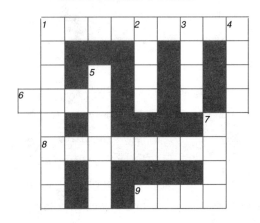

EXERCISE 2

Give *Student A* clues for each answer in *CROSSWORD PUZZLE 2* until *Student A* guesses the answer. Use "blanks" in your clues.

EXAMPLE:
STUDENT A: "What's 1 down?"
STUDENT B: "He's poor now, but I'm sure he'll be rich BLANK."
STUDENT A: "Someday?"
STUDENT B: "That's right!"

For help making clues, look at the *Preview* section of the unit shown for each word, but try to make up your own sentences.

CROSSWORD PUZZLE

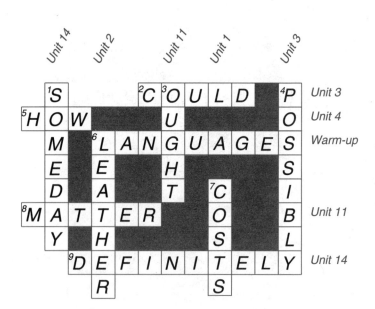

○ Memo ○
• ONLY THE STUDENT GIVING CLUES SHOULD LOOK BACK AT THE UNITS.
• YOU CAN GIVE MORE THAN ONE CLUE FOR EACH ANSWER.

TAPESCRIPT

John: Nice party, huh?

Maria: Yeah, it is.

John: Can I get you something to drink?

Maria: Uh, sure, thanks. Just a Coke, please.

John: There you go.

Maria: Thanks.

John: I'm John, by the way, John Fletcher.

Maria: Hi, I'm Maria Gomez. Are you a friend of Jack's?

John: Yeah, we used to be roommates.

Maria: Oh, really? Where are you from?

John: Denver, originally, but I live here in Chicago now. And you?

Maria: Oh, I was born just around the corner—and I still live here.

John: So how do you know Jack, Maria?

Maria: We teach at the same school—different subjects, though. I'm an art teacher.

John: That's interesting. I'm a graphic designer. I do magazine work and stuff.

Maria: Really? So you're interested in art...

John: Oh, yeah, very much. I love going to shows.

Maria: Me, too.

John: Oh, yeah? Have you seen the Picasso exhibit at the Art Institute yet?

Maria: No, but—

John: Listen, I'm going tomorrow with Jack and a few friends... Would you like to join us?

Maria: Sure, I'd love to.

John: And after that, we're all going to a terrific French movie—

Maria: Oh, I'm sorry, but I don't speak French.

John: That doesn't matter, I can translate for you—and anyway, it has subtitles.

Maria: Well, okay, that sounds great.

John: Terrific—um, would you like another Coke?

Maria: Oh, well, yeah, but... Is there any diet Coke?

Conversation One

Woman: Sure, Tuesday at four is fine. ...Right, okay. Oh, can I ask you one more thing? ...Do you know if I'll be able to eat afterwards? If not, I'll have a late lunch— ...I see, right, I didn't think so, okay, so I'll eat before I come. ...Uh huh, thanks again, bye-bye.

Conversation Two

Woman: Yes, I've looked everywhere—if you don't have it I guess I'll just have to order it. ...Well, do you know how long it'll take if I order it now? ...Two weeks, okay, and do I have to pay for it first, or— ...When I pick it up, I see. ...Okay, I guess I *will* order it now. Could you tell me how much it is, with tax and everything? ...Twenty-one sixty, okay— ...Sure my name is Sally Hill.

Conversation Three

Woman: Four hundred dollars?! I thought it was going to cost about two fifty! ...Yeah I know, I know, but could you tell me what costs so much? ...Uh huh...yeah...I see...okay, well, when will it be ready? ...Seven in the *evening*? ...Okay, Friday at seven—I'll be there. Oh, and, should I call first to make sure it's all done?

Conversation Four

Woman: And could you tell me what time it's over? ...Ten-fifteen, I see, okay, and how much is it? ...Eight fifty, right, okay. Oh, one more thing—do we have to get there early? I mean, do you know if there'll be a long line? ...No? Great, thank you very much.

Conversation One

Clerk: I understand, Miss, but we have a lot of those. Can you tell me what it looks like?

Woman: Well, it's very plain, with almost no design, and it's made of leather—soft brown leather. And it doesn't have a strap or zipper, just one little gold snap. It's a little larger than pocket-size.

Clerk: You lost it this morning?

Woman: That's right, about ten o'clock.

Clerk: Okay, just a minute, I'll see if we have it.

Conversation Two

Girl 1: Yeah, it came this morning—Daddy *told* us he'd send one.

Girl 2: Is it a nice one? What does it look like?

Girl 1: It's mostly black and it has a beautiful design all around it. And it has a nice little silver latch and little silver plates on the corners—it's really beautiful!

Conversation Three

Woman 1: Where did you get that? It looks just like mine!

Woman 2: Really? I bought it in Mexico. Is it exactly the same as yours?

Woman 1: Well, almost. Mine is made of leather, too, and it's the same size, but it has a longer, thinner strap.

Woman 2: Does it have these little leather strings on the front?

Woman 1: Yeah, just like that.

Conversation Four

Boy: What is it, Dad? Come on, tell me!

Dad: Your birthday is *tomorrow,* not today.

Boy: I can't wait! Just tell me what it looks like...please?

Dad: Well, it's small, and it's mostly made of plastic, and it has a little window, and some switches—

Boy: And it has earphones, right?

Dad: Okay, okay, go ahead and open your present.

Conversation Five

Man 1:   So, can you buy one for me while you're there?

Man 2:   Yeah, sure, but there are so many types. What kind do you want?

Man 1:   You know, just a plain brown one, made of *real* leather, of course. I like the ones with two locking latches—key locks, not combination locks.

Conversation Six

Woman: It happened just a minute ago! It was right next to me and now it's gone!

Policeman: Please, ma'am, calm down. What does it look like?

Woman: Well, you know, it's black, and it has a big lens—no case, just a lens cap, and a thin, black shoulder strap. Please hurry, officer! He'll get away!

UNIT 3	Listening Task	Page 18

Larry: It's going to be a great party Saturday night, huh Julie?

Julie: Yeah, but I don't know what I'm going to do—I have a million things to do this weekend.

Larry: Is there anything I can do?

Julie: Well, yeah, maybe. Do you think you could borrow your dad's car and take me shopping tonight? I have a thousand things to buy.

Larry: Well, okay, I guess so—anyway, I'll ask.

Julie: Great! Pick me up around six, and—oh yeah! Can you lend me thirty or forty dollars?

Larry: Of course, no problem. I have about sixty if you need it.

Julie: That'll be perfect, Larry, thanks. And after we go shopping, could you possibly pick up Gina and Marisol—

Larry: Gina and Marisol? But why—

Julie: —and Bonnie and Francine and Maggie?

Larry: Well, it's a small car, but...sure, I'd be glad to.

Julie: And listen, I don't have time to do that English homework this weekend, so I was wondering if you could possibly write a short essay for me, just a page or two?

Larry: Oh I'm sorry Julie, but I really have a lot of homework, and—

Julie: Oh never mind, it can wait, I suppose. But would you mind checking over my math homework? I did it at lunch.

Larry: Not at all. Tonight I'm doing *my* math homework, and—

Julie: Are you free tomorrow?

Larry: Tomorrow?

Julie: Yeah. Would it be possible for you to watch my brother Jimmy for an hour or two? I'm supposed to baby-sit after lunch, but—

Larry: I'm afraid I can't, Julie. I have basketball practice all afternoon. Sorry.

Julie: Basketball practice? But how can I get ready for the party if you can't do anything for me?

UNIT 4	Listening Task	Page 24

PART ONE

Conversation One

Woman: Excuse me, Miss? How can I turn on my reading light?

Flight Attendant: Just push this button here, in your armrest—the one with the little light bulb on it.

Woman: Oh yes, I see. Thank you.

Conversation Two

Man: Pardon me, ma'am, but could you tell me how to use these headphones?

Flight Attendant: Sure, just plug them in this hole here...that's right...and push this button to adjust the volume, and turn this dial to change the channel.

Man: Okay, I have it now—thank you very much.

Conversation Three

Flight Attendant: Would you like a blanket or a pillow?

Woman: Not right now, thank you. Maybe later.

Flight Attendant: Okay. If you need to call me for anything, just press this button with the little figure on it.

Woman: Oh, this one next to the light button? Thank you very much.

Conversation Four

Flight Attendant: We're serving dinner now, ma'am. Could you pull your tray down, please?

Woman: Oh yes, um, just a second...

Flight Attendant: First just turn that lever and then pull the tray down.

Woman: Yes, of course—there.

Conversation Five

Man: Excuse me, how can I adjust my seat?

Flight Attendant: Okay, first you press this large button on your armrest and hold it in. Then you just push back against the seat or lean forward.

Man: I see, thank you.

Conversation Six

Woman: Is this the air control up here?

Man: I don't know—excuse me ma'am, is this the air control?

Flight Attendant: Yes, it is. To open it, turn it clockwise, and to close it, turn it counterclockwise.

PART TWO

Conversation One

Woman: Where is that light switch again?

Man: Um, let's see...push that thing up there next to the light.

Woman: I thought I had to push a button in the armrest here.

Man: No, I think it's up there, next to the light.

Conversation Two

Man: That's right, dear, just plug them in that little hole there, then push this button to adjust the volume, and—

Woman: Don't I turn this dial to adjust the volume?

Man: No, she said push the button for the volume! Turn the *dial* to change the channel!

Conversation Three

Man: I push this button with the light bulb to call the flight attendant, right?

Woman: No, not that button. Push the other button.

Man: What other button? I thought it was this button with the little light to call her...

Woman: No, no, push that button *next* to the light button to call her.

Conversation Four

Man: I can't get this food tray out!

Woman: Just pull the tray down, dear.

Man: No, no, you turn this thing here first and *then* pull the tray down.

Conversation Five

Man: This seat won't go back!

Woman: Just press that large button and—

Man: I *did* press it!

Woman: —and hold it in.

Man: What? No, you don't have to hold it in.

Conversation Six

Woman: Dear, could you turn that air control thing clockwise for me?

Man: You want it closed?

Woman: No, open.

Man: Well, to open it you turn it *counter*clockwise.

Woman: WILL YOU PLEASE TURN IT CLOCKWISE!

UNIT 5   Listening Task   Page 30

Conversation One

Woman: Could you do it today, honey? I just want to go straight home and lie down—my head is killing me.

Man: Well, okay. How do you use the machine?

Woman: Just put everything in and make sure the door is closed tight. Then pour one cup of soap in the little compartment in the top, and put in six quarters.

Man: That's it?

Woman: Oh yeah—set the temperature to hot. Just turn the dial.

Man: Okay, no problem.

Woman: And do you think you could pick up some groceries on the way home?

Conversation Two

Woman: Excuse me, do you know what this is made of?

Salesman: Yes, I do. The outside is sixty-five percent polyester and thirty-five percent cotton, and the lining is made of one hundred percent nylon. The filling is one hundred percent down.

Woman: Does it have a hood?

Salesman: Yes, it does. Just unzip the back of the collar and pull it out.

Conversation Three

Lou: Excuse me, but I'm new here, and—

Nina: No wonder I've never seen you before.

Lou: Yeah, well, do you know how to—

Nina: My name is Nina, by the way.

Lou: Nina? Hi, I'm Lou, nice to meet you. Anyway, could you tell me how to use this? I mean, all these buttons...

Nina: Oh, sure. Just put your page in here, face down, dial the number, and press this button here.

Lou: I see, thanks.

Nina: Anytime. Um, would you like to see how to use the copier, Lou?

Conversation Four

Allison: Shawn, can you get my ski jacket and wool scarf from the hall closet?

Shawn: Sure...um, could you tell me what they look like? This closet is really full.

Allison: Oh, well, the jacket is light blue and it has a white lining, and the scarf has blue and white stripes.

Shawn: Oh, yeah, I got them...I think.

Allison: And could you see if my sunglasses are in the inside pocket?

Shawn: This jacket doesn't *have* an inside pocket, Allison.

Conversation Five

Woman: I'm looking for something small and light.

Salesman: Well, this one is very popular. As you can see, it has

all the necessary attachments.

Woman: I see...and how do you empty it?

Salesman: Just press this button here, remove the front cover, and take out the bag. Then just slip a new bag in and close the cover. It's very easy.

UNIT 6   Listening Task   Page 36

Conversation One

Friend 1: Okay if I smoke?

Friend 2: Sure, go ahead.

Conversation Two

Son: Is it okay if I use the new car tonight, Dad?

Dad: I'd rather you didn't.

Conversation Three

Man: Pardon me, I wonder if I could possibly use your phone?

Man: I'm sorry, but it's out of order.

Conversation Four

Brother: Hey, Sis! Do you mind if I borrow your laptop computer this weekend? I have a lot of homework to do.

Sister: Sorry, I'm afraid not. I have to use it.

Conversation Five

Girl: Can I go to a party Saturday night with Susan and Jenny?

Mom: Well, okay. But don't be late.

Conversation Six

Friend 1: Is it all right if I open this window?

Friend 2: Of course.

Conversation Seven

Friend 1: Mind if I turn off the TV? Nobody's watching it.

Friend 2: No, go ahead.

Conversation Eight

Man: Excuse me, Mr. Bellows. Would it be possible for me to take next Monday off? I have to take my sister home from the hospital.

Boss: Uh huh—that'll be all right.

Conversation Nine

Man: Hey, is it okay if I park here for a minute?

Man: Sure.

Conversation Ten

Student: Miss Riley, do you mind if I leave class early today? I have to meet a friend at the airport.

Teacher: No, not at all.

UNIT 7   Listening Task   Page 42

[*Class bell rings.*]

Mrs. Fenway: And don't forget to read Chapter Five and answer questions one through eight on page ninety-nine! Oh, Jonathan, just a minute—I have to speak to you.

Jonathan: Yes, Mrs. Fenway?

Mrs. Fenway: Jonathan, why didn't you answer the questions on the homework sheet for today?

Jonathan: Oh, I'm sorry Mrs. Fenway, but I read the wrong chapter last night.

Mrs. Fenway: Oh, I see But afterwards, why didn't you read the right chapter after you looked at the questions?

Jonathan: Well, I had to do too much other homework last night and I didn't have time.

Mrs. Fenway: Now, Jonathan, I'm sure you didn't have *that* much homework yesterday. You'll have to spend more time on your studies and less time watching TV.

Jonathan: Yes, Mrs. Fenway.

Mrs. Fenway: Also, your project partner, Amy, tells me that you haven't started your science project yet.

Jonathan: Well, I couldn't find the art supplies I need to build the volcano.

Mrs. Fenway: Come on, Jonathan, you can find those things in *any* stationery store. Besides, Amy has had no trouble finding her supplies.

Jonathan: I'll try again today, Mrs. Fenway.

Mrs. Fenway: Yes, you do that and let me know how it's going tomorrow morning—and by the way, why were you late this morning?

Jonathan: Oh, I had to walk to school because the school bus got a flat tire.

Mrs. Fenway: A flat tire? Jonathan, no one else was late to school today.

Jonathan: Yeah, well, I couldn't walk as fast as everyone else because I have a sore foot.

Mrs. Fenway: I see, Jonathan, okay. Well, hurry along to your next class or you'll be late.

Jonathan: I will, Mrs. Fenway. See you tomorrow. [*Sound of running feet.*]

Mrs. Fenway: Jonathan!

Jonathan: Yes?

Mrs. Fenway: Do not run in the hallway.

Jonathan: Sorry.

UNIT 8　　　Listening Task　　　Page 47

Bob: Somebody will find us. I'm sure they're already looking for us...they'll find us, right John?

John: I don't know—they may never find us. I think we should build a raft and the four of us should sail out of here.

Sue: I agree with John—we have to get out of here ourselves.

Bob: I don't think so, Sue. I believe we're all safe here. There's plenty of food and water. In my opinion we should build a shelter and wait to be rescued. What do you think, Mary?

Mary: I don't agree with you, Bob. We can't wait forever. We have to do something—but I think that just one of us should try to get help, and the rest stay here.

John: Actually, I think that it's too dangerous out there for one person...

Bob: Right, John, I think so too. In my opinion we should all stick together.

Sue: That's true, but we can't just sit here!

Mary: I agree completely, Sue... Well then, I guess we should *all* go together, like John says...

Sue: Absolutely! Let's start working on a raft!

UNIT 9　　　Listening Task　　　Page 53

Conversation One

Man: I like the style, but I'm not sure about the fit. Do you have a bigger size?

Salesman: Just a moment. Ah, yes. Would you like to try these white ones?

Man: Sure, thanks. Oh yeah—these are much more comfortable. I'll take them.

Conversation Two

Man: You want the red one, huh?

Woman: Yeah. It's roomier than the blue one.

Man: Well, yes, but it's not as sporty as the blue one.

Woman: That's true, but I like the extra space—you know, for luggage...and for shopping...

Conversation Three

Lisa: They're cute, aren't they? Which one do you like, Janet?

Janet: The one on the right, I think. He's much more handsome.

Lisa: Do you think so? I like the other one. He looks more mature.

Janet: Look—they're coming this way, Lisa! What shall we do?

Conversation Four

Travel agent: How long do you have in mind?

Woman: I'm not sure—could you give me some idea of the prices?

Travel agent: Sure. Let's see, the Bali tour is ten days—that's $2500.

Woman: Do you have anything cheaper?

Travel agent: Our Phuket tour is about $2000, but it's not as long. It's eight days.

Conversation Five

Woman: Oh, yours is much better than mine!

Man: No, not at all—I think yours is as nice as mine.

Woman: No, no, no, not really. Mine is not nearly as nice as yours. I love yours.

Man: Oh, well, thank you. Here, please take it.

Woman: Oh no, I couldn't.

Man: No really, I insist.

Woman: Oh goodness...thank you.

UNIT 10　　　Listening Task　　　Page 59

Conversation One

Man: In my opinion, Paris is much more expensive than New York.

Woman: I couldn't agree more, but a nice apartment does cost a bit more in New York.

Man: That's true, but everything else, like food, entertainment, transportation—

Woman: Absolutely, especially if you drive here. Do you? Drive, I mean.

Man: As a matter of fact I do. I'm parked right over there. Would you care to go for a drive this afternoon?

Woman: That sounds lovely.

Conversation Two

Husband: I don't know, this is much more expensive than a three-speed bike. What do you think?

Wife: I think he'd enjoy the car more now, but actually, he'll use the bicycle a lot longer.

Husband: Yeah, I think so, too. We can get the bike *and* a few other presents with the extra money.

Wife: That's true. How about a new car for me?

Husband: Not *that* much extra, dear.

Conversation Three

Angela: Frankie, how did you *do* that?

Frankie: It wasn't my fault! A kid on a bike shot in front of my car and I went up the sidewalk and hit a telephone pole.

Angela: If you ask me, Dad is going to kill you!

Frankie: No he won't—I'm going to get it fixed like new.

Angela: How much do you think it's going to cost?

Frankie: I don't think it'll be more than five hundred dollars. By the way, Angela, could you lend me two hundred dollars?

Angela: Ha!

Frankie: Come on, *please*?

Conversation Four

Simon: But Mom, why can't I get a motorcycle? Lots of kids in high school have motorcycles—and they're cheaper than cars...

Mom: Simon, I don't care about other kids. Motorcycles are far more dangerous than cars, and you are still a new driver.

Simon: But motorcycles are more fun, and they're easier to park, and much better on gas.

Mom: What does your father think?

Simon: Well...he said no. But if you—

Mom: I agree with your father completely. The answer is no.

Conversation Five

Miss Lee: Joshua, I didn't see you at rehearsal yesterday. Where were you?

Joshua: I'm sorry, Miss Lee, but my brother needed help fixing his car. I had to go straight home yesterday.

Miss Lee: Well, don't miss it this afternoon, okay?

Joshua: I won't, I promise. But Miss Lee, I was wondering if I could hand in the final paper a few days late. I have to go Christmas shopping with my sister this weekend.

Miss Lee: Well, okay, but no later than Wednesday—and don't miss any more rehearsals. The school play is next week, Romeo.

UNIT 11	Listening Task	Page 66

Jenny: So, Elizabeth, have you decided what to do for Sophie's graduation party?

Elizabeth: I don't know, Jenny. I'd like to do something *different*, you know, and surprise her.

George: Why don't you rent a limousine to pick her up and bring her to the party?

Elizabeth: A limo? No, I don't think so George.

Jenny: You know what? You ought to rent one of those huge wide-screen TVs and have music videos playing constantly for the kids. They love that.

Elizabeth: Music videos on a wide-screen TV—that sounds good, yeah—I'll do that.

George: And a live band, Liz, you should get a live band! I know these guys—

Elizabeth: Um, that sounds interesting George, but that might be a little expensive, and a lot of trouble to arrange and all that... No, I don't think so.

George: Oh. Well, how about a disk jockey then? I know this guy who's real good, and he's not expensive...

Elizabeth: Hmmm...yeah, that might be better. Music videos inside and a D.J. outside...let me think about it.

Jenny: Why don't you have fireworks in the evening—that'd be fun.

Elizabeth: Yeah, you're right, Jenny—Sophie loves fireworks! Good idea!

George: And sky-writing in the afternoon! You can hire a few planes, and—

Elizabeth: George—

George: No, huh?

Elizabeth: No. And it might rain anyway.

George: Oh, yeah, right. Well, maybe you'd better rent a big tent for the back yard.

Elizabeth: That *is* a good idea, George, but I'll have to see how much it costs first, and the size of the tent and everything.

Jenny: And if I were you, Elizabeth, I'd hire caterers to cook and serve the food—you know, one less thing to worry about.

Elizabeth: Caterers—yeah, that sounds like a good idea, too.

George: I know! How about a guy getting shot out of a cannon? You could put the net on one side of the tent, and the cannon on the other side, and...hey, where are you going?

UNIT 12	Listening Task	Page 71

[*Sounds of driving in a car.*]

Janet: Did you hear about the accident at this intersection last week?

Linda: Yeah, I saw it on TV. Pretty bad.

Janet: Have you ever had a bad car accident, Linda?

Linda: Yeah, a long time ago.

Janet: Really? What happened?

Linda: Well, I was driving with a friend in the city. We came to a red light and stopped in the right lane. There was a wall next to us, on the right. A really big truck pulled up next to us on the left. The light changed green, we started off, and the truck moved over to the right...and crushed my car against the wall. He just didn't see me!

Janet: Wow! Was anyone hurt?

Linda: No, we were really lucky—just scratched from broken glass. All the windows broke. When we stopped, the wall was on the right and the truck was on the left, and we couldn't get out of the doors! So we had to climb out through the windshield.

Janet: Gee, you *were* lucky—you could've been killed!

Linda: Yeah. Anyway, since then I've always been real careful of trucks, like that one up ahead.

Janet: And I bet you're not crazy about driving next to walls, right?

Linda: Yeah, right—like this wall coming up...oop, red light. [*Sound of truck.*] Janet, have you ever had déjà vu?

UNIT 13	Listening Task	Page 76

[*Telephone rings.*]

Mia: Hello?

Zachary: Hello, Mia? This is Zachary.

Mia: Oh, hi, Zachary, what's up?

Zachary: Oh, nothing much. I was just wondering—are you busy this weekend?

Mia: Well, a little. Why?

Zachary: Well, are you free on Friday? Would you like to see a movie?

Mia: I'd love to, Zachary, but I'm going over to Yuriko's Friday night—I promised. She has a cold and we're going to watch TV, you know, and talk.

Zachary: Oh, I see, okay. Well how about Saturday afternoon? How about going swimming?

Mia: I'm sorry, but I have a French class Saturday afternoon and I have to do a lot of homework before class.

Zachary: Oh, well, do you feel like going bowling Saturday night?

Mia: That sounds great, Zachary, but I'm going to a birthday party for a girl in my French class. Sorry.

Zachary: And I guess you're busy on Sunday, right? I mean, would you like to play tennis or something?

Mia: Well, I have aerobics class in the morning, and in the afternoon—

Zachary: Sunday night, Mia! Dinner! How about having dinner Sunday night? Or are you—

Mia: Sure, that's a great idea.

Zachary:	What?
Mia:	I said that's a great idea.
Zachary:	Oh. Really?
Mia:	Really. I'd love to.
Zachary:	*Oh, no...*
Mia:	What's the matter?
Zachary:	Sunday night I have to pick up a friend at the airport...
Mia:	Oh, well, maybe another time, then.

UNIT 14   LISTENING TASK   PAGE 81

Jack:	So tell me, Loni, is Harry all set?
Loni:	Yeah, we finished packing this evening.
Jack:	Where is he now?
Loni:	Out with some friends.
Jack:	I hope he doesn't come home too late. We have to leave for the airport at six in the morning.
Loni:	Don't worry, Jack, he knows. ...But I'm a little nervous about this whole thing—I mean, Japan is such a long way away.
Jack:	Come on, honey, it'll be a really valuable experience for him. He's twenty-two years old, he's a qualified teacher, and he speaks a little Japanese. I'm sure he's going to have a great time.
Loni:	But we won't see him for a whole year.
Jack:	That's no time at all—it'll probably be over in a flash. You wait and see.
Loni:	But what if he decides to stay there? He might meet a girl and settle down over there!
Jack:	So what's wrong with that? As long as he's happy. He'll keep in touch, whatever happens.
Loni:	But maybe he'll never come back!
Jack:	Then we can visit him in Japan, okay? Look on the bright side, honey!
Loni:	Well, okay, I'll try. ...Maybe we should start learning Japanese, huh?
Jack:	Now that's a good idea. *Arigato.*
Loni:	Harry got two what?
Jack:	No, no—I said "*Arigato*". That's Japanese for "Thank you". Harry's been teaching me a few words.

UNIT 15   LISTENING TASK   PAGE 87

Conversation One
Man:	So, how do you like it so far?
Woman:	Well, it's okay, but... Have you ever been caught in a storm?
Man:	No, not really. A little rain, maybe...
Woman:	Well, I think there's going to be a storm today.
Man:	Nah, it may rain a *little*, but I'm sure that there won't be a storm. [*Sound of thunder, followed by heavy rainfall.*]
Woman:	WE ARE GOING TO DROWN! WE ARE DEFINITELY GOING TO DROWN!
Man:	MAYBE WE'D BETTER ROW TO SHORE...

Conversation Two
George:	Good morning, Jenny. Hey, you don't look so good. What's the matter?
Jenny:	Oh, I feel awful! I have a terrible headache, and I'm so tired...
George:	Why don't you go home early? I'm sure the boss will understand.
Jenny:	Yeah, I know, but my desk will probably fill up while I'm out, and I don't want to get behind.

George:	If I were you, I'd forget about work for a day or two. You really ought to take the day off and—hey! Would you like to go hiking this weekend? I'm going to go to—
Jenny:	George, please, you've got to be kidding! Oh, my head...

Conversation Three
Woman:	I think I'd better—
Man:	Dear, let me do this, okay?
Woman:	But don't you think I should turn the water off first?
Man:	I've fixed drains a dozen times before. Could you hand me that wrench?
Woman:	Okay, but it might leak.
Man:	It'll be okay, could you just—[*Sound of gushing water*]—could you just turn off the water, please?

Conversation Four
Woman:	Let's do something different this weekend. We could go out. How about going to the beach?
Man:	It's going to rain.
Woman:	Oh, well, would you like to go rollerblading at the rink?
Man:	Nah, I've never done it before—I don't know how.
Woman:	Okay, then, do you feel like going to a movie?
Man:	Nah. Hey, we haven't been to the video store in a while. Let's rent a few movies...that'd be—
Woman:	Different, yeah, real different.

Conversation Five
Man:	See? It's not so bad, right?
Woman:	Why don't we set up the tent?
Man:	Come on, this will be great!
Woman:	I think we'll be eaten alive by mosquitoes.
Man:	I've never had a problem with mosquitoes. [*Sounds of coyote and bear in distance.*] Um, you're right. I think we'd better sleep in the car. Could you give me the keys?
Woman:	The keys? I don't have the keys! I thought *you* had the keys!